About Susan Swan

"A hip, 20th-century Dickens. . ." —*The Edmonton* ...

"Swan has a gift for the provocative . . . with her leonine presence, even her name, she should exude the musk of an outrageous literary Amazon. And yet what you are struck by is her earnest good heart." – *Mirabella*

"Yes, Swan seems to be saying, being trapped inside one's body is lonely; other people can be twisted, can even maim and kill . . . but let us drape these nightmares in outrageous costume. Let us turn them into Halloween. Even if only for a night."
– *The Globe and Mail*

"The stories in [*Stupid Boys Are Good to Relax With*] bring comic relief to the rapidly changing area of dating and relationships." – *Prairie Fire*

"If her teaching methods are as lively as her writing, she must have some of the happiest students in Canada." – *The Expositor*

Praise For Susan Swan's Previous Work

"With singular comic panache and rare poignancy . . . *The Wives of Bath* is a thoroughly modern tale of shifting sexualities. It is also extremely funny. Swan writes with rare verve and flare."
– *The Sunday Times*

"A highly entertaining read." – *Montreal Gazette*

"Exhilarating . . . clarifying . . . double-edged pleasure."
– *Saturday Night*

". . . a touching, suspenseful, often hilarious tale."
– *Publishers Weekly*

Susan Swan

Stupid Boys Are Good to Relax With

SOMERVILLE HOUSE PAPERBACKS

Canadian Cataloguing in Publication Data

Swan, Susan
    Stupid boys are good to relax with

A Patrick Crean book
ISBN 1-895897-73-4 (bound)   ISBN 1-894042-38-7 (pbk.)

I. Title.

PS8587.W345S8   C813'.54   C96-931110-9
PR9199.3.S935S8

Originally published in 1996 as
A Patrick Crean Book / Somerville House Publishing

Book design: Gordon Robertson
Cover art: Tamara de Lempicka "Kizette en rose"
        Cliché Ville de Nantes—Musée des Beaux-Arts—B. Voisin
Author photograph: Joy von Tiedemann

Printed in Canada

Published by Somerville House Publishing,
a division of Somerville House Books Limited,
3080 Yonge Street, Suite 5000, Toronto, Ontario M4N 3N1
Internet: sombooks@goodmedia.com
Web: www.sombooks.com

Somerville House Publishing acknowledges the financial assistance of the Ontario Publishing Centre, the Ontario Arts Council, the Ontario Development Corporation, and the Department of Communications.

For my mother who taught me to love

and my grandmother who believed
life was a romance

The well-being of the world needs women's sexuality and enjoyment, relieving female sadness.

– Barbara G. Walker, *The Women's Dictionary of Sacred Symbols and Objects*, 1988

I used to love the theatre, the long, passionate tragedies on stage, all that drapery. But I much prefer the intermissions. Don't you? Little half-glimpsed dramas in the foyer, comedies d'amour *that last a few seconds.*

– William Beckford, from *Una Visita a Fonthill Abbey*, by G. B. Spalleti, 1840

Romance is an old word for story.

– Vera Frenkel, from the program notes for *Mad for Bliss*, 1989

Contents

Gutenberg Stories

Cyber Tales

Gutenberg
Stories

Sluts

IT WAS Tom's contention that you could spot a slut by the colour of her complexion. The slut was the one with white skin. Not off-colour white or alabaster like the skin of heroines in old novels. But sickly white. White as chalk or a cadaver.

There were two women with chalk-white skin in Madoc's Landing and everybody knew they slept around. The first was Mellie Sommers, an unwed mother who lived in the old captain's house on First Street. The second was Mary Lou Heller who shot her husband through the eye with his Colt .38.

Tom said it wasn't sex that produced the tell-tale colour, but poor living habits. Sluts were girls who could stay out late because nobody cared about them. They weren't like us. They could eat plates of french fries soaked in brown oily gravy and drink cherry Cokes without anybody reminding them to eat their vegetables.

Tom and I grew up in Madoc's Landing, and so did my friend Kim. Kim's mother was Bernadette and Tom said she was a slut too, only she was an exception to the rule because she had a healthy complexion. Bernadette's last name was Dault. Nobody in my family could say the French word right. They pronounced it "dalt," which sounds like "dolt" with an *a* instead of an *o*, but I said it like "dough," the way it was meant to be said.

Madoc's Landing is a hilly Canadian town settled by a mix of French and English. It is located at the bottom of a bay belonging to the second largest of the five Great Lakes. In 1951, when I lived there, the Canadian National and the old Canadian Pacific Railway met in Madoc's Landing. It was the biggest town in Tecumseh, an Ontario county, with a population of 6,123. The judge of Tecumseh and the Crown attorney came from Madoc's Landing and we were the attorney's children. Every morning, Tom and I watched a big, dark man in a Homburg hat back his Chrysler Airflow out the driveway. This man was our father, Tiff Quinn. He wheeled the car sharply onto Second Street, then squealed the tires in front of the nuns' house on the corner. He was always in a hurry to get to the assizes.

When his taillights vanished over the Fifth Street hill, Tom and I crossed Second Street to pick up Kim. Her mother kept house for the nuns in exchange for food and lodging. Kim's father was "missing"—which is how my mother put it.

When Bernadette saw me at the door, she didn't call me by my first name, Julie. Instead, she sang out to Kim, "Here she is, *mon petit chou*—Tiff Quinn's daughter."

The year is 1953. Tom, my father and I are posing for a photograph in the backyard of our house on Second Street. We're standing by the cedar hedge where the barn used to be before Dad tore it down to hide all trace of the buggy horses he kept behind the house like a farmer. The snap was the first photograph taken with my Brownie. It was taken by my mother, Marjorie Quinn. You can see the outline of her short, wavy shadow falling across Tom and me. She had forgotten to follow my father's instructions. She has taken the picture without checking the position of the sun.

It is summer but my father, Tiff Quinn, is wearing a white shirt and bow tie and baggy flannel pants. The cuffs break on his shoes, which is the way Canadian men wore their trousers then. He is also dressed in his black court robes and one of his hands still holds the glass of gin my mother had just poured him. His other hand is on my shoulder, pulling me against him. I'm the dark-haired girl in a skirt that is far too short for me, and Tom is the owlish, fair-haired boy in a cowboy hat. His glasses spoil the western look he aims for but nobody wants to tell him that. Tom is fourteen and I have just turned eleven.

The snap was taken the day my father had obtained a conviction against Mary Lou Heller. Mary Lou claimed her husband, Frank, had shot himself by accident while cleaning his gun, but my father persuaded the jury that people don't shoot themselves in this way. Nobody looks down the barrel of a gun when they clean it. Frank, who ran the ambulance service in Madoc's Landing, knew about guns. Skeet shooting was one of his hobbies. And the coroner found powder burns on Frank Heller's left hand, as if he had been trying to ward off a gunshot. My father argued that Mary Lou had murdered her husband, twenty years older than herself, as they sat drinking a cup of afternoon tea.

Of course, the evidence against Mary Lou was circumstantial. It shouldn't have been possible to convict her. But every piece of evidence is a thread, my father said. And if you gather enough threads together, you can make a hanging rope. The photograph of Frank Heller and his grotesquely shattered eye was one thread. It was taken by a Kodak Pony, a better camera than my Brownie Hawkeye. Tom stole the photograph from my father's briefcase and showed it to me. I saw Frank slumped in a chair, looking at me as if he were asking for help. One eye was open and the other eye, the bad eye, was dark and evil, a bloated bag with a rip in the middle. The defence argued that the photograph was inflammatory but my father pointed out that the photograph was not retouched or shot in a special light. The picture was a piece of objective evidence. The photographer hadn't tried to make anything more than what the camera saw.

Mary Lou had also persuaded Frank to take out an insurance policy on his life eighteen months before his death. That was another thread. And when Mary Lou moved her boyfriend in two months later the threads became a rope, just like that.

The year is 1955, winter. Kim is eleven years old and I am thirteen. Kim is posing for the first colour photograph I will take with my Brownie Hawkeye. I will put it on the first page of my new album. (On the first page of my old album, I put the black-and-white picture of Tom and me with our father.) The new album is a black book tied with a piece of matching black cord and inscribed with the simple title "Photographs." It is winter in the snapshot. You can see the snowbank rising like white frosting in front of our big turreted house on First Street. The banks also rise on either side of the cleared walk leading up to our large red-brick porch with the half-moon Palladian window above our front door.

Kim, my first real best friend, is in the foreground, disguised as a fat person in a padded brown snowsuit. She is patting my dog, Joe, and she is wearing my favourite flowery cotton print. I've loaned her the dress to go to mass in, but my gift is hidden under Kim's suit, which swells around her arms and legs.

Behind Kim, a woman in a hideous pair of sealskin galoshes and a raccoon coat is striking a pose, one hand on her hip. She is standing next to Tom, who is not wearing a coat, only a Maple Leaf hockey sweater, and he is staring at Bernadette as if he wants to make it clear to me and anyone else who sees her that Bernadette is the third-most notorious woman in Madoc's Landing, next to Mellie Sommers and Mary Lou Heller. The important thing to notice about Bernadette is the colour of her cheeks. They are as pink as tea roses.

Tom said Bernadette was a slut, no matter how much rouge she wore. For one thing, Bernadette was French-Canadian and she wore skirts so tight you could crack a flea on them. For another, she dyed her hair a listless ochre, so it looked like dyed sheep's wool.

It was my contention that Tom's evidence was only prima facie. That is, it put a responsibility on Bernadette to explain herself but it wasn't enough to convict her. Tom said he was glad I was making him back up his argument, because every time we fail to make the Crown prove its case, we are all a little less free.

"Tom," I said, "you may be the Crown and I may be counsel for the defence, but Bernadette is not a slut because she is a good mother to my friend Kim. I'm sure," I said, "sluts don't take care of their children." Of course, I had no way of knowing how well Mellie Sommers treated her baby girl in private, but I guessed by the way she slapped her kid's hand when it cried in its stroller, shrieking and pointing at the Coke bottle Mellie was always drinking from, that Mellie didn't deserve to be a mother.

As for Mary Lou Heller, she didn't have any children, so there was no point speculating. But Tom said being a slut didn't have anything to do with children, it had to do with men, with sex, with spreading your legs for every Tom, Dick and Harry. The dictionary didn't mention Tom's meaning for the word *slut*. Our Oxford said a slut was a slattern or slovenly woman. But Tom said untidiness was not the point either.

The point was you couldn't trust a slut. A slut did the dirty deed with anybody who asked her, a slut rolled in the hay with all the boys, only she didn't get paid for it. A prostitute was a slut, but a slut wasn't a prostitute because a slut wasn't in it for the money. A slut was worse than a prostitute. She was too stupid to know she could make a living at it.

Tom said I shouldn't get on good terms with sluts. It was tricky enough that I was a Protestant whose best friend was a Dogan, a Mick—i.e., a Catholic.

Of course, he said, he had no worry about me in the slut department. "I know you'll never be one," he said. "You're just like Mother, you're not interested in sex." Still, he told me I had to be careful; I was too sympathetic. I should stay away from girls who had double-barrelled names like Mary Lou Heller, and wore V-neck angora sweaters that smelled of Shalimar, a perfume Mom called "whore's lure."

Tom also told me there were many kinds of sluts and not all of them lived in Madoc's Landing. For instance, Anne Boleyn, the wife of Henry VIII, was a slut. So was Zsa Zsa Gabor, the movie star, who married every Tom, Dick and Harry she slept with so she could pretend she wasn't a slut. Then there was our mother's cousin, Lulu Marsden, who lived in Vancouver. What else could you be with a name like that? You couldn't be a lady with a name that rhymed with cuckoo, could you?

"Are sluts capable of ordinary living?" I asked. "Do they sometimes eat mashed potatoes instead of french fries, and use a Brownie Hawkeye?"

"Of course, sluts act normal," Tom said. "That's how they fool you. But if you could see what they do when everybody goes to sleep," Tom added, "you would find out that sluts are every bit as disgusting as you thought."

It is Monday, one day after I took my first colour photograph of Kim and Bernadette. Tom and I are hiding behind the lumber pile at the end of the nuns' yard. Bernadette stands by the back door, hanging out the washing.

It is a cold overcast afternoon late in March, the time of year when the spring sun should be melting the snow into gurgling streams along Second Street. But spring is nowhere to be seen and the icy wind blows Bernadette's scarf behind her back like a banner. The wind also makes our cheeks turn red and our noses run. We don't complain. We are used to being disappointed by the weather.

In our shiny thermal jackets, Tom and I crouch behind the lumber, listening to the creak of the clothesline as the accused strings up the garments.

You slut.

I say the word to myself to test the sound of it. In my mouth, it sounds slushy, like the popsicles Mom doesn't like me to eat in the house because they turn into cylinders of soggy ice when I suck on them.

Slut, slut, slut.

It also sounds like "rut," which I know is a bad word. Deers rut and have baby fawns like Bambi. Sluts rut and their skin decays, turns white like the lumpy paste I use in school to stick my cut-out pictures onto bristol-board posters.

This afternoon, Bernadette's arms move stiffly as she hangs up the nuns' old, mended sheets and tea towels with the insignia "Madoc's Landing—The Gateway to the Great Lakes." It is so cold the feeling is seeping out of my toes. This familiar sensation does not scare me. I know I can stamp my plastic rubbers on the ground and scrunch up my toes to keep the blood flowing, but it's a nuisance to do it.

Then Bernadette hangs up something small and red. Tom pokes me and I look hard to see what it is. It's a pair of panties. Now she hangs up two panties that are named after the days of the week . . . Friday and Sunday, and one pair in black lace that makes me think of spiderwebs. The panties disturb me. I have peeked into my mother's lingerie drawer and seen with my own eyes that her underwear was snowy-white, every piece, from the all-purpose brassières to the baggy nylon panties in the style of shorts.

Then Bernadette hangs up a black band supporting two bulbous red cups. Tom utters a strange, puffing hiss beside me. "Ssss . . . slut," he says, and I feel a little quake of angry excitement. In his mouth, the word slut sounds like "slice." It comes out sharp and spins across the yard towards Bernadette like a hunting knife. I wait for it to strike her in the throat, for Bernadette to fall to the ground, but Bernadette couldn't have heard him because she keeps on hanging her underwear up.

Now she strings up a garter belt and then a small flannel nightgown that belongs to Kim. Bernadette picks up the wicker hamper and stops. She is looking right at us, at the lumber pile. We crouch down even more and lower our heads in their knitted toques.

"Kim!" she calls. "Are you there, *mon petit chou*?" Tom puts a mittened hand on my knee so I won't move. Kim is playing behind the Catholic church on Third Street. There is no chance Kim will hear Bernadette's cry.

At last, Bernadette puts her empty laundry basket on her hip and kicks at the door of the old shed at the back of the nuns' house. It creaks open and she disappears. Tom's hand is still on my knee. We continue to crouch behind the pile of lumber. Our breath makes foamy clouds in front of our mouths. Finally, Tom lifts his hand off my knee and stands up. He moves sluggishly towards the clothesline. Then he nods at me and I begin to march back and forth, patrolling the yard. One by one, Tom removes the wooden clothes-pegs from the soft garments. He puts the pegs in his mouth and hands the underwear to me. Together we waddle back behind the pile of wood.

There, we squat, going over the clothing of the accused. The underwear astonishes me. It's see-through, flimsy. I sit next to Tom, examining the scarlet brassière. Its red cups are fringed with circles sewn in black thread like the concentric circles on a dart board. Nesting inside the cups are two rubber falsies.

Suddenly, Tom hisses. The pair of black lace panties come apart in his hands, broken. He shows me how they fold together again so the crotch is intact.

"Is that so she doesn't have to take her pants off to tinkle?" I ask, and Tom looks at me in disgust—because, in my shock, I have used the baby's word for pee. He takes off his mittens so he can open the panties again. "It's for the man, silly," he says, his mittens dangling from under the cuffs of his snowsuit on a piece of yarn. "So he can poke it in."

"Oh," I say, "oh," and then I think, Slut, slut, slut—all the better to rut, rut, rut.

Tom unzips the front of his snowsuit and takes out my Brownie Hawkeye. He doesn't look me in the eye. Instead, he waves his hand to indicate that I should display the evidence so he can take a picture. I crouch down and arrange the underwear on the snow. Then I pull myself to my feet and pad slowly over and stand behind Tom. He doesn't look up, he's kneeling so it's easy. I lean down and push Tom as hard as I can from behind.

There isn't time to look for my Brownie Hawkeye. Panting, I grab the bra and panties and run down Second Street to the Hellers' house. It stands alone behind an empty school and nobody lives there now because Mary Lou's in jail and Frank is dead. The house is clapboard and dirty white like the snow except for the red trim around each of its narrow windows. I look closely at the front windows to make sure nobody is in the house. Then I count three breaths and go into the little yard behind the house where Frank Heller grew his vegetables. A few withered stalks of corn poke up through the icy ground.

The cornstalks were planted by a dead man, I think. Then I remember the photograph. What did he think when he saw Mary Lou pointing the gun at his face? Our father said the gun was fired only five inches from his left eye. Frank couldn't have suspected her or he wouldn't have let her come that close. Did Mary Lou sidle up to him, pelvis first, wiggling her hips as she pointed the gun in his face?

I put my hands on my hips and stick out my tongue. "Nana-nana-nana—Frank Heller! The worms crawl in and the worms crawl out—up your gizzard and out your snout."

Now I scoop up a handful of snow. To my surprise, it sticks to my mitt. It's packing snow. A soft, heavy spring wind is blowing now from the south. I pack the snow into each cup of the brassière. I press it in firmly. I hook the brassiere up the way my mother hooks up hers. I put it on backwards so I can work the clasp. For a moment, two breasts stick out the back of my snowsuit. Then I slide the bra around to my front. It slides easily because my snowsuit is slippery. Now the cups protrude from my chest, and I have a bosom, a great big snowy bazoom. I stand in front of the side window and shake my breasts at the Hellers' old house.

"Slut, slut, slut," I shout.

A few minutes pass. I sit down in the melting snow, among the dead cornstalks. The snow under the bottom of my padded suit feels wet. Soon it will soak all the way through, leaving a big wet stain, but I don't care.

"Nana-nana-nana—Mary Lou! You're a slut who likes to rut, rut, rut!" I begin to dig purposefully behind the old stalks. The effort makes my snowsuit feel heavy and hot, but at least the warm wind is making the snow soft. I keep on Bernadette's enormous brassière until the very last. Then in it goes, right to the bottom of the hole with the rest of Bernadette's things.

All at once I sit up and stare again at the old Heller place. I am sure Frank Heller is in there, spying on me, not with his single open eye, no, of course not. Spying on me with his torn, bloated one. I hold my breath and wait for his raging voice. Wait for the word to come spinning and tumbling right at me.

Slut!

The sound I hear is very small. I hear it all around me. The sound of icicles dripping from the boughs of the tree next to the Heller place, and from the eaves of the broken porch. Nobody is in the old house, no one. Not a single soul is watching me from those icy, still rooms, or huddling near me among the old cornstalks.

I am all alone in the March twilight and I feel as sad as you can possibly feel.

I roll up a large wet ball of snow and place it over the top of the hole containing Bernadette's underwear. I could make a snowman, but I don't have a carrot for a nose. Or small pieces of coal for the eyes. Besides, Tom used to help me with my snowmen. And it's not much fun to make one by yourself.

Stupid Boys
Are Good
to Relax
With

MAYBE you've never realized this before, but stupid boys are good to relax with. You don't need to do much except smile encouragingly as they try out their authoritative manner on you. Meanwhile, you get to think about the really interesting things that matter. Like the face at the window.

I saw the face at the window again last night. Cross my heart and point to heaven, I saw it staring right back at me through the glass slats my stepmother Sal turns down to protect my modesty. My father, the surgeon Morley Bradford, has reported it to the hotel management, but I don't think he believes me because my stepmother says I'm making it up. "Young girls will do anything to get attention," I heard Sal whisper to Morley back in their bedroom. "And Mouse is no exception. She's still flat as a board and dying for boys to notice her."

Trust Sal to put her finger on a sore spot. I must be the only underdeveloped girl in Nassau. You wouldn't give me a second look if you walked into the Fort Charlotte Beach Hotel and saw me sitting here listening to the calypso band with Sal and Morley. It's easy to miss me. My body is as flat and seamless as a worm's except for my left shoulder which is slightly rounded, so I wear a T-shirt over my bathing suit or a loose-fitting blazer, like the one I have on now. I have told everyone at the hotel I am fifteen and a half but I am really only thirteen and one-quarter and I have no curves—I mean my body is just a tube of skin that ends in a ball of tight brown curls which spring, after a bath, *boing-boing* from my head.

Frankly, there is nothing positive you can say about an underdeveloped bust although I have met a woman here who has no breasts and gets away with it. Her name is Monique, our social director. She's the woman who wears her platinum hair in a French chignon even when she's water-skiing. Monique is the sexiest woman at the Fort Charlotte Beach Hotel. The sight of her makes Sal grumble, "What's that woman got I haven't got twice over?"

I want to laugh in my stepmother's face because it's obvious there's a little more to having sex appeal than owning a pair of breasts. Even Morley's old dead eyes look up with interest when Monique saunters by in her tight silver bathing suit, one hand to her neatly pinned-up chignon in case a gust of wind catches her unawares.

Cynthia, the girl from New Jersey, says I shouldn't worry because any day now I will get my period and it will make zigzaggy female hips and breasts burst through my baby fat — just the way Moses hit the rock of Horeb and brought forth water for the thirsty Israelites.

Cynthia is sitting at the table with me, and so is her brother, Jonathon Allerton Cushman Jr., whose crew cut is shaved so close to his scalp you can see spaces between the hairs, like the fur around a kitten's ears. Jonathon and Cynthia and I are drinking Cokes and watching the swimmers in the vision-level glass pool. We like sitting here because we can stare at the swimmers' bodies, especially the fat or ugly ones, without anyone getting mad at us.

Behind us, the bartender is making my father a cocktail with a name that rhymes. Bahama Mama. His jigger clanks and froths as if it wants to say: *Hey there, Dr. Bradford! Slurp me down! It's happy hour, time to have a party!* But Morley's too pooped to hear the voice of the Bahama Mama. Morley wouldn't like me telling you this but he hasn't sat in the sun since the day we arrived. He sleeps all day instead.

Poor old Morley. He looks like Dr. Kildare on the wrong TV set. Any second from now, the lids will close on his smoky blue eyes and Morley will start snoring.

I have Morley's eyes which Sal says are prone to showing circles of fatigue. Only my eyes are not dead, but moist and alert—constantly darting here and there like the bodies of the lizards that shimmy away from my father's new wing-tipped shoes when we walk to our bungalow under the hibiscus trees. My name, by the way, is Mary Beatrice Bradford but everyone (except Morley) calls me by my nickname—Mouse.

"Is Dr. Bradford okay?" Cynthia says and Sal leans forward and jiggles my father's arm.

"Morley, please!" Sal says and Morley swings his big grey head up and around as if he didn't know where he was for a minute.

"They're playing our song," Sal says.

Morley yawns and slowly shuffles to his feet.

"See you later, Mary Beatrice, Cynthia and—" Morley looks at Sal.

"Jonathon Cushman the second," Sal says.

"Jonathon Allerton Cushman Jr.!" Jonathon says. "I am Jonathon Jr. and my father is Jonathon Allerton Cushman Sr. It's the way we say it, sir, in the U.S. of A."

"Is that so!" Morley smiles sleepily and puts one of his big surgeon hands around Sal's waist and I turn again and look at the vision-level pool because there is nothing in the world more embarrassing than watching parents dance.

"I never see your dad swim," Jonathon says when Sal and Morley are in the middle of the floor. "Doesn't he know how?"

Frankly, for a boy, Jonathon Jr. is not that smart. Although he is sixteen and three-quarters, and owns a red Triumph sports car that costs sixty cents to the gallon, Jonathon still cleans his glasses like a baby— i.e., he doesn't breathe on the lenses like Sal and then wipe, so the lens won't smear. Instead he crumples up his cocktail napkin so the wrinkles on it make the dolphins in the hotel logo look crabby and then

Jonathon dips the napkin in his drink and rubs his glasses with it.

"My stepmother says Morley doesn't like sand between his toes."

"Of course her father knows how to swim," Cynthia says.

"What happened to your mother?" Jonathon says.

"She died of a brain tumour when I was four."

"That must be why he lets you call him Morley," Cynthia sighs. "I wish we could call our dad by his first name."

"Don't be dumb, Cynth." Jonathon jerks his closely shaved head towards the dance floor. "Mouse, you wanna—?"

"Who would want to dance with you?" says Cynthia. "You've got sweaty palms."

I stand up so quickly I almost lose my balance, but Jonathon doesn't notice. He just grabs me by the waist and pushes me out onto the floor where everybody is bobbing around to the calypso music of the Great Sparrow. All the women here are gaga about him, even Sal who sucks in her funny little tummy if he walks by. To tell the truth, I am just crazy about the Great Sparrow myself. He whistles at Cynthia and me when we are together at the pool, working on our stupid-boy sayings. It's part of a handbook we are going to publish when we are grown up.

A stupid boy, in case you didn't know, is usually between the ages of twelve to twenty-two, but older boys can be stupid too. Cynthia, who is fifteen and three-quarters, says Jonathon is a stupid boy on account of his bragging. For instance, he is always telling Monique, the water-ski instructor, and anyone who will listen, how he learned to get up on one ski when he was twelve while Cynthia still has to start with two.

I don't know if the face at the window is a stupid boy, but I'm afraid he might just be one because he does nothing except stand outside my bungalow when nobody is watching and stare in.

I saw the face the first time by accident. In the middle of the night, a noise woke me. I jumped up and opened the glass slats on my bedroom window. At first, I couldn't spot anybody in the gloom. I looked and looked, and then just before the tennis court, I saw a bulky figure shuffling like a zombie under the hibiscus trees whose blossoms I like to put on my pillow.

It was Morley.

He held his black leather doctor's bag in his left hand like a big purse. Then he turned off the path and I heard a door shut in the southwest wing, which is ringed with spidery white balconies that make me think of the tiers on a wedding cake. I counted the balconies and then I counted the doors, waiting for Morley to reappear. Then I gave up and went back to bed and began to touch myself.

I only touch myself when I'm sure Sal is asleep. Otherwise, she'll stick in her head at just the wrong moment and say, "Are you all right, Mouse? Your breathing sounds strange." Frankly, I don't think Sal touches herself or else she wouldn't blunder in on me the way she does and ask stupid questions. I always say, "Yes, I'm fine," and go right back to it after she leaves.

The first time is usually the hardest. It can take up to eight minutes. Then it's all downhill after that. Not that I mind. I like doing it when it only takes sixty seconds or so, one after another, easy as pie. I can have over a hundred when I get going. That night, I was on number twenty-three when I looked up and saw the face staring at me through my window. I didn't hear a sound to warn me it was there. You see, the face didn't make as much noise as Morley who must have slammed the door on his way out. And the truly unbelievable thing is I wasn't scared, even though I'm afraid of all the things a girl like me should be afraid of — i.e., bats, spiders, snakes, mice and *not* getting your period.

My light was out so all I could see was an inky oval shape the size of a football. And a pair of shoulders in a red T-shirt. Cross my heart and point to heaven, I saw an inky head move from side to side, as if the face was trying to get a better look at me. I faked a little scream, and the next thing I knew my door was rattling and I heard Sal shouting: "For God's sake, Mouse! Are you all right?"

Sal couldn't walk very well when I let her in, plus her eyes rolled crazily inside her mask of cold cream, but she was still sober enough to pat me on the cheek and tell me to go back to sleep and forget about what happened.

"I'll get Morley to take care of it," she said sighing. Only she didn't because the face came back again the very next night.

Where am I now? Oh yes. On the dance floor with Jonathon. You see how effortless it is to think of interesting things when you are with somebody who doesn't expect you to do or say anything important. But please don't get me wrong: I feel grateful to Jonathon for his stupidity. It means I don't need to care about making a faux pas, which is a nice word for *bungle*. I can just go ahead and let him talk without a worry in my head.

"Mouse?" Jonathon says.

"Yes?" I reply.

"Do all Canadians live in igloos?"

"I'm afraid so."

"Jeez, that's terrible!" Jonathon says. "Do you have to travel by dogsled too?"

I nod politely. There's not much point shattering the fantasies of somebody like Jonathon. He doesn't know much about anything except how to address the son of a man with the same name or what it costs to fill up a sports car in the U.S. of A. But he does have the greatest president in the world: John F. Kennedy, who winks at you on the TV. I like the way President Kennedy hurries laughing up the steps to Congress so people don't notice his sore, stooped back.

I also like the way he never looks pooped. In his photographs, he's always smiling at his daughter Caroline, who is allowed to do handstands in his office and sit next to him in his sailboat.

Behind Jonathon's shoulder, I can see the swimming pool lit with underwater lights and every so often the turquoise wall turns silver with air bubbles when a swimmer jumps in. But nobody's watching the pool any more because the hotel guests are having a wonderful time dancing to the music of the Great Sparrow. And that includes Jonathon and me.

The second time I saw the face I didn't scream. For one thing, it was late, almost half past ten, so I was sleepy and, well, more relaxed. Naturally, I couldn't see a pair of eyes or a nose because the glass slats got in the way, but I saw a big pink circle which got wider and wider, and smack dab in the middle of the circle I saw something quivery. It took me a few seconds to realize that the face was smiling at me and the quivery thing was the face's tongue! I had my light on, you understand, so it was hard to see what was out there in the dark.

At first, I admit, I felt a little panicky. I wasn't undressed yet but all the clothes I'd worn for the last two days lay on the floor. I got up and began to straighten things out because I didn't want the face to know how messy I was. I picked up my bathing suit, which was still wet from my swim, and rolled it into a ball and threw it into the bathtub.

Then, carefully, I folded up a pair of shorts and hung them on the skinny hotel hangers which come apart if the clothes are too heavy. I spied a pair of underpants on the floor of the closet and stuffed them into the pocket of my blazer. I did a few other quick touch-ups, but nothing too major because I was starting to realize the face couldn't tell on me.

In fact, how my room looked was none of its business.

So I gave up and just left the other three pairs of shorts lying on the rug. Then I lay down on my bed and wiggled under the sheet. I took off my blouse and pedal pushers, but I didn't take off my underpants or my T-shirt because I didn't want the face to see my rounded shoulder. Then I peeled off the sheet and pulled up my T-shirt on my good side so the face could see my right breast, and outside my window I heard somebody say, "Aaah!"

I yanked down my T-shirt and pulled the sheet back up to my neck.

Some things are better left to the imagination, aren't they?

By then, I was sweating quite a bit because it was very humid, even though Sal had opened all the glass slats of my window to let in a breeze. Cross my heart, it must have been a hundred degrees. So I closed my eyes and tried not to think about the heat. I mean, I tried to concentrate on Kookie, the actor from 77 *Sunset Strip*. And soon I forgot about the face because I got carried away picturing the funny little tilt of Kookie's head when he combs his D.A. I usually don't like boys with greasy hair: Elvis Presley is just a big drip as far as I'm concerned, but Kookie is different. Kookie doesn't shake his pelvis like a stirred-up rattler; he moves very very slowly, and naturally, so it feels as if he's stepping right out of the TV, you know . . . walking up to you and pulling you close for the big clinch and then his nice, smiling mouth is on yours, and you feel his body (the bottom half, of course) press against you and your own skinny body starts melting into his hips and then he lays you very slowly down and then . . . well, just as it started to happen, I realized the face was making a really weird garbled noise.

At first, I was too carried away to listen properly. And I didn't exactly want to hear what the face was saying. There wasn't anything wrong with seeing the face, but I knew I'd get into trouble if I started having conversations with it. So I didn't say a word. A second later I heard the sound of feet hurrying off the veranda of our bungalow. And I realized the face had been asking me to open the door and let it in.

Over by the bandstand, I can see Morley, the very person who should be doing something about the face, mouthing the words to "Yellowbird." In fact, Morley's lips are opening and shutting like Faye, my goldfish, when I need to change the water in her tank. Now I spot something really strange. Yes, believe it or not, Morley's old dead eyes are looking right at me! And I know what he's thinking—Mouse is having herself a whale of a time. So I smile at Morley and try to look happy, although it's a little tiring dancing the cha-cha with somebody like Jonathon who has to make every step as elaborate as he can so people will admire him.

At least a millisecond of recognition from my father is better than nothing. It happens now and then. Like today on the tennis court when I aced my serve. I sent the ball sizzling sideways into Cynthia's court and Morley called from his chair on the sidelines: "Hot diggity dog, Mary Beatrice!" I hate it when Morley uses his old-fashioned expressions or calls me by both my first names.

As I came off the court, Morley smiled at me in the saddest way and I realized—surprise, surprise—Morley wishes he was me! You might ask, why did my father want to be me when there is nothing about me to attract him? But it wasn't me he admired. Only my youth. For a moment I felt hopeless. Mouse—get it right, I told myself. Your own father will never notice you. He's only interested in himself and Sal. And I felt glad I'd caught him out in his envy. Superior even. I thought, Ha-ha! Thirteen against fifty-seven. I win—you lose!

Oh, I beg your pardon. I have to pay attention. Jonathon is whirling me so fast I can hardly keep up. Now we are doing the cha-cha in front of the bandstand, and I almost lost my balance again. Just as I get myself steady on my feet, I look up and see Cynthia dancing all by herself in front of the Great Sparrow who is stretching out his arms towards her in his big Batman sleeves.

"I bet that Negro can't get up on one ski like me," Jonathon mutters. "He probably doesn't even know how to swim."

Jonathon says "Nigra" for Negro, which is what Americans from the South call people with dark skin. Jonathon is from New Jersey. I think he said it to be mean. We are Canadians and we pronounce the word "knee-grow."

"How do you know?"

"Very few of the Negroes here swim," Jonathon says. "They are too backward." Jonathon leans close and something wet and slobbery, like worms, touches my cheek.

Double ugh. If this is one of life's finest pleasures, kissing must be overrated because it doesn't make my ears hot or me wet in the place I can't speak of here.

"Mouse?" Jonathon sounds scared. "Don't you like me?"

"I told Sal I'd be back to our bungalow by nine-thirty."

Jonathon sighs.

"Okay," he says. "I'll walk you home."

I don't like the way Jonathon says Negro and I don't like the expression "too backward" either. But I guess you can't expect much from a stupid boy who always says the wrong thing because he is trying to impress people. Anyhow, I let Jonathon hold my hand on the path under the hibiscus trees. It doesn't mean a thing to me although his hands are pretty sticky, just like Cynthia said. But I can't tell him that. You have to let boys like

Jonathon down easy because their egos aren't built to take the truth.

At the door, I say good night and Jonathon looks sad but I'm smiling because I'm going to see the face. Unless it's already been and gone. Or maybe it's not going to come at all. Maybe it's cruel like Morley who knows how much I want his attention and can't make himself give it. Naturally, I've wondered what the face would do if I let him in. He might very well be a bit nasty. He might put matches between my toes and set them on fire. Or twist my arms behind my back in a wrestling hold like Whipper Billy Watson. Or maybe he'd take me off to his shack and chain me to the bed like the man who put a girl in a coffin and kept her there for two years. I can't help wondering if he let her get up to pee as much as she needed to and I worry about how embarrassed she must have felt getting him to buy her sanitary napkins.

There's no way of knowing for sure, is there? Suddenly, I hear a *bap-bap-bap* at the door of our bungalow, as if somebody is excited to see me. And then I understand: the face wants me to let it in.

I fumble around but my door is locked (I always lock up after coming in—just like Sal). The rapping is getting louder and right at the bottom of the door, where I have opened a few slats to let in the night air, I spy a pair of large, plain-stitched leather sandals.

This makes me fumble even more, and when I am finally able to swing the door open, who do I see standing on the step of my bungalow but the Great Sparrow himself.

"Chil', I'm sorry . . ." Behind the Great Sparrow's head, I can see the hibiscus blossoms tossing in the evening breeze.

"Your pa's goin' to the hospital with Miss Bradford. They sayin' it's his heart."

I don't move or speak. I just stand there thinking about how the Great Sparrow leaves off the endings on words the way our teachers say we aren't supposed to do.

And all of a sudden I start to sob, and the Great Sparrow gently takes my arm and we go slowly off down the long path to the hotel under the hibiscus trees. I think about Morley lying as if asleep in some dumb ambulance and how I am already starting to miss him and I wonder if he will ever miss me. And for no good reason, I trip over my own two feet and the Great Sparrow catches me and squeezes me up against him. He holds me so close I can hear his heart thudding like far-off thunder, and I think, Morley's heart is stopping while my heart, and the heart of the Great Sparrow, are ticking on.

This makes me too scared to speak, so I just stand there and let the Great Sparrow hug me. He's pretending it is the kind of hug you give somebody who needs comfort, but I think it is the other kind, only I couldn't swear on it because I've never had that kind, not from Jonathon or anyone. Now the Great Sparrow says something against my neck in a voice so whispery I wonder if he really wants me to hear, and then I can't see the stars in the dark night sky or the hibiscus trees whose flowers Cynthia and I love to pick because I'm squeezing my eyes tight, tight, trying to remember the first time I saw the face so I'll know if it was the Great Sparrow at my door, but I can no longer picture now how the face looked, or if there was even a face at all.

Dear Cynthia Allerton Cushman

Dear Cynthia:

You find some funny stuff in old cupboards. Always worth keeping. Movie mags from the 1950s with Elvis kissing Ann-Margret. Turquoise hula hoops, a cardboard tiara. And old diaries. In this case, it was my Grade Eight scribbler with "The Stupid Boy Handbook" you and I composed the year our parents took us to Nassau for our Easter vacation. I have sent it along to amuse you.

As you might guess, I have a lot of time on my hands these days. I am pregnant—it's my first—and working part time in the medical library near the university.

I remain, yours truly,

Mary Bradford (a.k.a. Mouse)

The Stupid Boy Handbook

---

*Why a handbook?**

A handbook is what girls like us need now. With lots of instruction. Cross our hearts and point to heaven, we will not tell you one false word because the ways of stupid boys can take most girls, on the average, a lifetime to learn.

IF THEY ARE LUCKY.

---

* Recommended reading for ages twelve to twenty-two

What is a stupid boy?

A stupid boy is between the ages of twelve to twenty-two and he is usually:
   a) a guy who thinks he's grown up when he's not
   b) a guy who thinks everybody is SO crazy about him he can treat you like garbage
   c) a guy who takes himself TOO seriously to be taken seriously

Stupid boy love techniques

1. For openers, sticking his tongue down your throat.
2. Drinking stale beer through his nose.
3. Greeting you with a farting noise made by cupping his hand under his armpit.
4. Lighting a blue angel[*] to get your attention.
5. Burps just before he tries to kiss you.
6. That's it—those are all the techniques they know.

---

[*] Lighting a fart with a match

Stupid boys can fool you

If you are not careful, stupid boys can fool you into thinking you're going to be the one to change them. Only, you're not going to change a stupid boy and YOU KNEW IT ALL ALONG.

Even stupid boys can learn something

Even stupid boys can learn something from our handbook, although we're not making any promises.

Some useful facts about stupid boys

1. You can spot a stupid boy a mile away because he says things like: "Hey, Ma! Sandwich!" "Hey, you! Coke!"
2. Most stupid boys will always be stupid boys (except for the ones who are just going through a stupid-boy stage).
3. Stupid boys usually learn how to behave from their stupid-boy fathers. (But there are always

exceptions that prove the rule.)

4. Stupid boys are a good thing to give up for Lent. (Chocolate is much too pleasureable.)

5. If you share your Smarties with a stupid boy, he'll eat up every last one and accuse you of pigging out.

6. Stupid boys like stupid girls, but prefer smart ones who have temporarily lost their common sense; i.e., a smart girl who thinks she can change a stupid boy for the better. (Now that's emotional quicksand for you!)

7. You can't blame everything on stupid boys, but you can blame a lot more stuff on them than your mother said you could.

8. If you hang out with stupid boys too long, you become a stupid girl.

9. Stupid boys are like a good commercial. They give you a nice break to get ready for the main attraction.

10. Stupid boys are not everyone's cup of tea. There are still plenty of sensible girls left in the universe.

11. Stupid boys have been known to try to pass themselves off as men. BEWARE!

12. It's easy to spot a man who is a stupid boy because he will talk on and on and on about himself and not ask one question about you.

Stupid boys in the kitchen

1. Don't go near it.
2. Expect you to be impressed when they make
   a) beans,
   b) peanut butter sandwiches and
   c) *la pièce de résistance* — grilled cheese sandwiches with ketchup.
3. Throw out the spaghetti pot so they don't have to clean it.
4. Stick empty milk cartons back in the fridge.
5. Put the electric kettle on the burner.

Stupid boys are energy suckers

Stupid boys suck up ALL your energy until nothing is left but a pathetic little thing that used to be you. So carry this handbook with you AT ALL TIMES and refer to it often.

Body parts of stupid boys

1. Hot, sticky hands that don't let go. YUK!
2. Arm muscles that bulge as big as their Adam's apple.
3. Thighs as skinny as chicken legs.
4. A bum you wish you had.
5. Elbows sharp as slide rules.
6. Eyes that only watch hockey pucks and base-ball bats.
7. A mouth that says everything . . . except what you want it to say.
8. I don't know about the rest—yet. (And I'm not sure I want to find out.)

A *hundred ways to get rid of a stupid boy*

1. Tell him you want to grow up and be just like his mother.
2. Put on weight. It never fails. (Well, hardly never.)
3. Burp when *he* tries to kiss *you*.
4. Use your imagination—act boring.

5. Go out with boys who aren't stupid.
6. Tell him you've got your period and ask him if he would buy you a box of sanitary napkins.
7. Tell him you don't go past second base.
8. Repeat everything he says twice and then laugh like Woody Woodpecker.
9. Tell him he looks just like one of your heroes. THE MONSTER FROM THE BLACK LAGOON!
10. Ask him the meaning of the word triskaidekaphobia, and when he says he doesn't know the answer, shake your head sadly and say, "That explains everything."
11. Chew old toothpaste tubes and tell him you are suffering from a mineral deficiency in your diet.
12. Never change your socks and ask him to give you a foot massage.
13. Turn your back on him while walking away and say, "Here's a message for you." See if he's smart enough to figure it out.
14. Give him an address on Lake Titicaca and tell him you'll see him there.

15. Suck your finger and stick it in his ear.
16. Tell him you never see him in your dreams. Only your nightmares.
17. Go around singing hymns. If he asks you a question, stop, smile and say, "I'm training for the convent!"
18. Tell him you can't stand short, bald, red-haired men. If he says he isn't one of these, tell him you know he is going to grow into one sooner or later.
19. Give him an earthworm every time he says hello. Make it clear you keep worms on your person at all times. When he asks why, say, "I just love slime. Can't you tell? After all, I'm with you."
20. Squint like Clint Eastwood and whisper all of your favourite four-letter words. (Although this could turn him on.)
21. When the sun is out, wear a yellow slicker, tightly buttoned, and matching galoshes. When it rains, go without.
22. Flush his hockey cards down the toilet.
23. Tell him you can't wait to try out some of his favourite pastimes on him; i.e., what he does

to frogs and cats. Stick a lighted firecracker up his bum, and then laugh your head off.

24. Use his secret stash of *Hustler* magazines as fire starter.
25. Ask him to join the prayer group with you at your local church/synagogue.
26. Tell him you've fallen hard—for his best friend.

(Okay, so we don't have our list up to a hundred ways yet, but we know there are many, many more ingenious tricks for getting rid of a stupid boy, so just add on your favourite method here and it will be welcome news to girls the world over. Write c/o: Stupid Boy Handbook, Post Office Box #14, Petrolia, Ontario, Canada.)

Nobody Calls Them Servants Anymore

*Sometimes I see what Willa did
as a film clip*

SOMETIMES I see what Willa did as a film clip: Willa tilting the teapot over my grandmother's lap and my grandmother's hands up in surprise, her mouth open like Marilyn Monroe in *The Seven Year Itch* when the wind from a subway vent blew up her skirt. And other times I don't see anything at all. Instead I hear the slushy sound of Earl Grey tea falling onto my grandmother's lap. The falling tea makes a noise like somebody peeing on the carpet, except it's scalding hot, and under my grandmother's wool skirt is my grandmother's skin.

A *useful history of Willa's life as a servant*

Nobody calls them servants any more, but there were people like Willa Jackett all over the place when she went to work for my grandmother in 1930. It was the start of the Great Depression, but the Bradfords always had household help and they weren't about to stop on account of economics, which was the government's fault anyhow. So my grandfather, R. B. Bradford, made some adjustments and Willa became the fifth girl to help my grandmother, Daisy Bradford, raise her three six-foot sons in Petrolia, the old oil town near the Canadian shore of Lake Huron. What did Willa do? She did everything. Willa rose at 6.15 a.m. and put on the crisp white uniform my grandmother liked her to wear. Then Willa went downstairs and drew the curtains. If cards had been played the night before, she put away the tables and dusted and then she boiled my father and his brothers their three-minute eggs. Willa had to cook three meals a day and keep the house clean and, most important, be agreeable.

When my grandmother hired her, Willa was seventeen and she lasted thirty-one years before she upended
the teapot on my grandmother's lap. Willa was a Free
Methodist and she liked fads, old hymns and the midget
wrestler Little Beaver whose real name was Lionel
Giroux. When Willa wasn't going to prayer meetings,
Willa liked to watch him on television. Willa claimed
the newspapers were wrong—Little Beaver didn't come
from St. Jerome, Quebec, but had grown up on the
Ipperwash reserve on Lake Huron, like her. My grandfather, or R. B. as everyone called him, said there wasn't a
word of truth in what Willa told me. R. B. told me I'd
taken after Willa because I liked story-telling, but he
pointed out that I should be careful not to imitate Willa
in other ways. For instance, Willa saved Canadian Tire
coupons but always forgot to cash them. So R. B. traded
them in to buy new rakes for the vegetable garden he'd
planted right next to the old Bradford oil field which nobody worked any more. R. B. also used the coupons to
buy Willa nylon bobby pins and Willa's favourite
wrestling magazine and pairs of cheap fuzzy earrings
made of feathers which he said a woman like Willa enjoyed. (He would never buy feather earrings for my
grandmother, R. B. said, because she was strictly the

pearls type. I don't know what type he thought Willa was because he didn't say specifically.)

Willa wore the earrings when she did the gardening, and my grandfather said it was a wonder somebody didn't report a large Indian in a beret and sunglasses and feather earrings stealing the Bradford vegetables. My grandmother said Willa had no clothes sense but I thought Willa looked cool, like a jazz musician, and I was glad someone so strange had come to live with my grandparents because nobody, when you got right down to it, could hold my interest like Willa did.

How the trouble started

The day the trouble started Willa was forty-eight, twenty-five years younger than my grandmother who no longer looked young at all, although everybody said my grandmother's pompadour of silky white hair made her a double for Winston Churchill's wife. And I was thirteen, not the grown woman I am now.

Willa was sashaying slowly towards the television set, carrying a bowl of sugared strawberries, as red and pointy as tongues.

Just as Willa's big backside blotted out my grandmother from my view, Willa tripped over the television
cord. And Little Beaver, our favourite midget wrestler,
shrank to a dot of light.

"You sloppy girl! W-W—Wh—" My grandmother
turned to me—"What's her name, dearie?"

"Willa," I said. "Her name is Willa."

"Willa—that's right!" my grandmother said. "Willa
must be thinking about a beau. Plug in the—" My
grandmother made a restless gesture with her hand.
"Mary Beatrice, you know the word I mean."

"The TV."

"That's it. Do it now, dearie, and never mind W-
W—"

"I'll do it, " Willa muttered.

Now I knew Willa did not and *never* would have a
boyfriend as long as she lived. Willa had tripped over
the television cord because the villainous Fuzzy Cupid
had put Little Beaver, Willa's cousin four degrees removed, in a stranglehold on the ropes. Fuzzy Cupid
was breaking the rules right before our eyes and the referee was doing nothing about it. I started to say something along these lines to my grandmother but Willa
shook her head at me and plugged the cord back in.

Nobody spoke as the little pinprick of light blossomed into Little Beaver duck-walking out of Fuzzy Cupid's tiny hands—and oh heavens, no—sneaky old Fuzzy was belly-rolling into a double somersault! When Little Beaver turned, Fuzzy kicked him right on the side of his shaved head.

"You bum! You sidewinder!" Willa yelled and we both squealed as Little Beaver sagged to the floor, but my grandmother only flapped her napkin at Willa and said in her I-can-say-anything-I-like-to-Willa voice:

"Is *she* still here? Where is our—now what's the word I want . . . ? It's not S-H-I-T-E, I can tell you that. You—!" My grandmother turned to Willa and mimicked lifting a glass to her mouth. "Bring in what I'm telling you and be smart about it."

Willa stomped off to get the hot drinks, her big white leather shoes squeaking on my grandmother's oak floor.

"There will be no more television for—!"

"Willa," I said. "She's worked for you thirty-one years."

"I know that!" my grandmother cried. "But I won't have what's her name shouting and carrying on like that!"

"Gran," I said. "You always let Willa watch before."

"And what a mistake that was too!"

I didn't know what to say to that and a few minutes passed without either of us speaking. When I was little, my grandmother sang "Oh, my darling Clementine" at parties and everyone liked to stand next to her just to hear my grandmother laugh. But after she fell and broke her hip, my grandmother's memory had started to go, and there was just no point arguing with somebody who—one minute later—couldn't remember what had made her mad in the first place.

Related by landscape

The day Willa scalded my grandmother with her own tea, Willa had on her starched white uniform and she'd coiled her flat black braids like a schoolgirl's around the dome of her strange head. I use the word *strange* because Willa had a harelip which was almost as bad as my rounded left shoulder. R. B. told me Willa didn't get her lip from polio the way I got my bad shoulder. A harelip is a congenital fissure and has nothing to do with disease, let alone combs, or hair spray, but is spelled the same way as the other word for rabbit.

R. B.'s explanation only confirmed what I suspected: Willa and I were related by landscape. Willa had a fissure or valley and I had a hill or hump. Nothing my grandparents told me could convince me otherwise. In my heart of hearts, I worried it was Willa in her white uniform who had given birth to me and not my poor dead mother whose photographs were kept out of sight.

After I ate up every one of my strawberries

After I ate up every one of my strawberries, my grandmother rang the engraved silver bell on the table in the sun-room. It made a high, clear tinkling sound, which was how my grandmother laughed before the troubles started with her hip. And Willa squeaked in again on her white shoes and set down before me a cup of Neilson cocoa with melted marshmallow topping.

"Where did *you* put *my* tea?" my grandmother asked.

Willa just looked at my grandmother the way Fuzzy Cupid looks at his opponent before he slingshots him into the corner. And swaggered off.

Willa didn't come back.

"Can I go and get your tea?" I asked.

"No, sir! You sit right here!" my grandmother said.

My grandmother tinkled the silver bell again, and when Willa still didn't return, my grandmother pressed her foot on the buzzer under the carpet, the buzzer she'd once refused to use because my grandmother said it hurt Willa's ears.

In the kitchen, I heard the horrible static of its bell grinding over and over.

"Where is that bad girl! Get in here—oh, you know who I mean, dearie," my grandmother said.

"Willa," I sighed.

"Willa, come back this instant!" My grandmother stopped pressing the buzzer and thumped the floor with her cane.

Meanwhile, Fuzzy was holding Little Beaver in a hammerlock and Little Beaver wasn't getting up.

And the referee was pounding the mat with his hand, yelling the final count.

"One! Two! Three . . . !"

And then, just as I was giving up all hope for my hero—Willa lurched through the sun-room door.

"Looks like our boy's winning, Mary Beatrice," she said.

And sure enough, flying across the screen, for all the world to see, sailed Little Beaver—airborne and triumphant, his strong little legs and feet heading right for the dimpled chin of Fuzzy Cupid.

Willa smiled as she set down my grandmother's silver tea service on the table next to the engraved silver bell.

"I'm glad to see you're agreeable again, whatever your name is," my grandmother said. Willa nodded and then slowly, slowly, with the languor which so infuriated my grandmother, she lifted up the teapot from the tray and opening the lid slightly she began to pour.

R. B. stands for Rupert Brooke

My grandfather's real name was Charles, but he'd wanted to be a poet so his family called him R. B. after Rupert Brooke, the British poet whose sad poems about World War One I had to memorize in school. R. B. was deaf as a doorpost, and even though he liked poetry, R. B. had his problem side. For instance, he'd gambled away the last of the oil money, which wasn't very much by the time he got his hands on it, and he'd once been opposed to my grandmother hiring Willa.

"Jesus, Daisy! You're not going to hire one of them!" he said when Willa applied for the job as my grandmother's housekeeper.

"Don't you dare hold Willa's skin colour against her," my grandmother said. "Willa's a good girl and she's moving in tomorrow."

R.B. didn't complain about Willa after that although he did manage to point out that Willa's habit of watching the wrestling on TV was vulgar. My grandmother said there *definitely* was something trashy about those big, brutish men grabbing each other, but she wouldn't listen when R.B. said the matches were rigged. My grandmother said no wrestler she rooted for would cheat, and every Sunday afternoon she watched the televised matches with Willa and me. I sat on a pillow on the floor of my grandmother's sun-room and leaned my back against my grandmother's swivel chair and Willa sat on the kitchen stool, which she pulled up close to the TV because Willa's eyes were poor. Willa was too vain to buy herself glasses, my grandmother said.

After the wrestling was over, Willa would get out her guitar and sing *Oh, my darling Clementine, you are lost and gone forever* . . . until all three of us were weeping and then my grandmother would stop Willa and hug her. "There's nothing like a good cry, is there, Willa?" my grandmother would say and Willa would smile and let herself be hugged.

"Oh, Mrs. B.!" Willa used to exclaim. "You're going to look like such a doll in your coffin!"

Now this might sound like an insult to you, but coming from a religious woman like Willa, it was a supreme compliment.

Why my grandmother liked Yukon Eric

My grandmother always rooted for the big male wrestlers like Yukon Eric who drove a pink Cadillac and shot himself outside the church he was married in, and she was also just fascinated by Gorgeous George who had more muscles than most men, even if he was a homosexual. "I like manny men," my grandmother said. "And you and Willa would too, if you knew what was good for you!"

But Willa liked Little Beaver because he wore moccasins and a real Indian headdress and a buckskin jacket and I rooted for Little Beaver because he was short like me. I also rooted for the female midgets like the Fabulous Moolah and Karen Kellog and Dolly Darcel, but my grandmother said women shouldn't wrestle and I don't know what Willa thought because she wouldn't say.

The first noise I heard

The first noise I heard after the slushy sound of the falling tea was a high pitched *eeeeee-eeee*. For a moment, I thought it was Willa laughing, because R. B. always said Willa laughed like a stuck pig, but that was no help to me because I didn't have a clue what a stuck pig sounded like.

It wasn't Willa who was doing the screaming anyway. It was my grandmother as she ran out of the TV room. As for Willa, she just stood there holding the teapot, not making a sound. At least, if Willa was going to scald me, I was wearing my uniform for Bath Ladies College because I was going back to school that night. My tunic was made of thick rough cotton and underneath I wore purple bloomers and cotton underpants, so I knew I was in better shape then my grandmother, whose habit of not wearing any underpants under her skirt was a well-known sartorial tic among us Bradfords. My face must have had some effect on Willa because Willa put the teapot down, and then lowering herself as best as somebody like Willa can, she sat down in my grandmother's comfy chair and began to watch television.

What do you do in the middle of a war?

Nobody tells you what to do when you're in the middle of a war between two people you love, but somebody should make a study of it and recommend a few steps for people who find themselves in this embarrassing position. Should you be an isolationist or should you be a peacekeeper? Or should you roll up your sleeves and get right in the middle of it?

When I was thirteen, I hadn't understood the difficulty of this position before. In fact, I didn't pay attention to the way things had deteriorated until R. B. pointed it out to me, and after that I couldn't help seeing the signs everywhere. For instance, my grandmother would try to make Willa pick the vegetables for Sunday dinner on Sunday morning instead of letting

Willa go off to teach her early-morning Sunday school class. Willa didn't like to do the vegetables on Sunday mornings. She wanted to pick them in the afternoon, but Willa never refused my grandmother anything.

The Golden Rule was the reason Willa figured you shouldn't ask anybody for anything directly—you had to do it by performing little courtesies and considerations that end up being very influential. Because if you were nice enough, well then, other people had to be nice too.

So Willa would just stroll along after my grandmother in the garden, and whatever my grandmother pointed to with her cane, Willa would bend down and snap it off with R. B.'s old gardening shears. I liked to hide in the cedar hedge so they couldn't see me, and take snaps of them with my grandmother's Kodak when they were too absorbed to notice.

The sight was very interesting. My grandmother staggering on her walker past the six-foot statue of Pan which R. B. had given her after the birth of my father. She didn't want to stumble and break her hip again, so my grandmother was not looking at the horizon where you could see the last of the metal derricks sticking up in the old Bradford oil field next to the Catholic church. She was looking at the ground beneath her canvas walking shoes. And behind her swaggered Willa in her old navy coat and her beret and sunglasses, not to mention the dangling feathered earrings R. B. had bought for her. I knew Willa wore her white uniform under her coat so she would be ready to get my grandmother's lunch when she came back from church.

A *human being grows slower than a rose*

Willa didn't need to move too fast to keep up with my grandmother who lurched around her garden, getting madder and madder because she kept forgetting the names of the vegetables she wanted Willa to pick.

And the slower my grandmother went, the faster she wanted Willa to go. You wouldn't think a war would start over something like speed, except now that I'm older I know speed is more dangerous than anyone realizes. Frankly, speed is the most damaging idea I have come across, next to progress and enlightenment. My grandmother used to say people never change while R. B. claimed that people evolve. And I will go along with R. B. on that except he left out two important facts. A human being grows slower than any creature in the

universe. I'm serious. We are the slowest growing creatures around, slower than dogs and roses. It can take a
century just to learn to say, No, I don't want to cut the
vegetables now, and maybe an eon or two to believe you
deserve something better than a job in my grandmother's house.

And then, when we've finished growing up, we start
growing backwards, going down-down-down again, like
my grandmother, to the earth.

What I saw next

This is what I saw next after Willa scalded my grandmother with her own tea: Willa, rocking in my grandmother's swivel chair and watching the wrestling
champ Whipper Billy Watson on TV. When Willa noticed me standing there, she pointed to the floor of the
sun-room and I sat down beside Willa and I watched
TV too. Even though I could hear my own heartbeat, I
watched for at least seven whole minutes, sitting on the
floor, and neither Willa nor I spoke one word to each
other. But we did cheer and say things to the TV. For instance, when Gorgeous George stepped on Whipper's

hands, Willa booed, "Crush him! Kill the bum, Whipper!" And I said, "Go, Whipper Bill!" That was the first crazy thing I did.

I did several other crazy things

I did several other crazy things after Willa poured the tea on my grandmother's lap. I did nothing when my grandmother hollered, "Somebody! Please! Help me!"

Willa didn't move a muscle but I could not resist the shouts and groans of my poor grandmother who I knew, by then, had forgotten both our names, so finally I got up and slowly, slowly, like Willa herself, I walked down the hall and opened the door to my grandmother's bedroom. And there she was lying doubled up on her old four-poster, a pitiful heap of hair and bone. Her nylons were sagging around her ankles and my grandmother no longer resembled the ex-prime minister of England's wife although, thank God for both our sakes, her skirt was still covering her hips.

I gasped and the bundle on my grandmother's bed made a little croaking sound.

"Is that you, dearie?" it said. "Get—you know—!"

"R. B.?" I said.

"That's the one," the bundle started to sob. "And tell him—tell him—that woman nearly killed me."

I found my grandfather upstairs reading True Detective

I found my grandfather upstairs reading *True Detective*, and when I told him what had happened, he threw his magazine halfway across the room. It landed by my feet and, before we ran downstairs, I just had time to see the headline about Mrs. Evelyn Dick, the Hamilton adulteress who had sawed up her dead husband and used one piece of him for a doorstop, although for the life of me I cannot remember now just what piece of Mr. Dick it was.

My grandfather threw open the door of my grandmother's bedroom.

"Jesus wept, Daisy!" he shouted. My grandfather always shouted because he couldn't hear and he thought that meant you couldn't either. "What have we here!"

"Get what's her name out of my house!" my grandmother cried, and then she shrieked so loudly that

Willa must have been able to hear all the way from the TV room: "I never want to set eyes on another god damn Indian as long as I live!"

R. B. made a shushing noise and said as long as my grandmother could swear like that, he knew my grandmother wasn't dead yet.

And then my grandmother asked me to bring her some water and baking soda and I brought her baking powder instead of soda, and that ended up making her sting worse than ever in the place Willa had wounded, the very place my grandmother, with her love of pretty pastel suits and big-chested men, wouldn't want to get hurt in at all.

R. B. called up Sadie the nurse on the fat black kitchen phone and told her to send over an ambulance, and then R. B. ordered me to stand guard on Willa who was still sitting where I left her in front of the TV. Willa looked up as I came in and said, "Can you help me move this chair closer to the set, Mouse?"

"Sure," I said. "The wrestling match is nearly over anyhow."

"Afraid so," Willa said, and we both sat down in front of the TV just in time to see Whipper Billy Watson push the cart with Gorgeous George. "Push the cart" means holding somebody's legs off the floor like you are holding wheelbarrow handles, and when men do it to each other, it looks very weird and interesting.

When the commercials came on, R. B. was standing behind Willa.

"Listen, old girl," R. B. said almost softly. "You'll have to pack your bags."

"Oh, Mr. Bradford!" Willa cried. "Don't make me go!"

"Eh?" He cupped his ear with the hearing aid.

"Don't make me go, sir!"

"Willa, I have no choice," R. B. cried. "I can't let you stay here now." R. B. frowned and looked at the floor and Willa sighed and waddled off and the ambulance man walked in. His name was Arnie, and we all knew him because he went to Willa's church.

"I gave Mrs. Bradford an ice pack," Arnie said. "In a day or so, she'll be as good as new."

"Any bad burns?" R. B. asked.

"Only first degree," Arnie said. "Nothing to worry about, Mr. Bradford."

Then Willa came back, and R. B. and me and Arnie—we all stared at this stranger who was no longer in the starched white uniform my grandmother made her wear but a shiny polyester pantsuit. Willa had also undone her thick, flat braids and now her hair hung loose and free over her large shoulders. And, of course, she had on the feather earrings and her old pair of sunglasses.

She made a shy little coughing noise and held out something shiny towards me.

"Can I give this to Mary Beatrice, Mr. Bradford?"

"Yes, Willa, but no more funny business," R. B. said. I knew but nobody else did that it was the eight-by-ten glossy I liked of Little Beaver in his full Mohawk and his snappy leather jacket and moccasin slippers.

So I accepted the photograph and stood stock-still while Willa kissed me.

"Are you going to prison, Willa?" I asked and R. B. cried, "Mary Beatrice, will you just shush!"

"I'm taking Willa to the hospital where they know how to treat people like her," Arnie replied.

"Over my dead body, Arnie!" Willa said and almost ran — that is, Willa walked as fast as Willa could over to the statue of Pan in my grandmother's garden and threw her arms around it. She started to sing.

"Onward, Christian soldiers, marching as to war, with the Cross of Jesus going on before!"

R. B. pushed Arnie out the screen door and latched it. "Watch out, son!" he yelled. "She's off her rocker!"

Arnie sauntered past the petunias and the geraniums over to Willa.

"At the sign of triumph Satan's host doth flee!" Willa screeched.

"I can't get her arms loose!" Arnie called. "You'll have to help me, Mr. Bradford!"

"Can't!" R. B. cried and tapped his chest.

Arnie put his hand behind his ear and R. B. smacked his chest hard.

"Bad ticker!" he bellowed. Arnie waved and went over to the ambulance and pulled out something white from its back door. Arnie held it high over his head and marched over to Willa as if he was stalking a butterfly with a net. Willa looked around just in time and Arnie put the jacket behind his back.

"Onward, then, ye people! Join our happy throng," Willa shrieked.

"Willa! Stop that!" My grandfather banged the screen door. "Be a good girl! Do what Arnie says!"

"Blend with ours your voices in the triumph song!" Willa yelled.

Arnie shrugged at my grandfather and put the restraining jacket down. He whispered something to Willa and then he began to sing.

"Christ, the royal Master, leads against the foe, forward into battle, see, his banners go." Arnie stopped for a breath.

"Onward, Christian soldiers, marching as to war," he sang.

"With the Cross of Jesus going on before," Willa cried.

Arnie and Willa threw back their heads and intoned, "Amen!"

Then Willa let Arnie steer her over to the van, and when Willa couldn't step up easily into the front seat because she was so heavy, Arnie pushed Willa's great big bottom with his shoulder and once she was settled inside he locked the door.

Willa stared over at the house as if she hoped I was there watching but I don't think she could see either R. B. or me because both of us were still hiding behind the veranda door. When Arnie started up the motor, my grandfather put his arm around me.

"Everything's going to be all right now, Mary Beatrice," he said. "Just you wait and see."

Arnie drove past the statue of Pan in R. B.'s vegetable

garden and down through the old oil field where the derricks stood rusting among the hay crop, and I thought I saw Willa waving from the passenger window but I couldn't be sure because by then I was crying too hard.

Mouse Bradford—fifteen years later

Isn't it a dirty trick to jump ahead like this? But I have to tendril into the future so you will know what happened to Willa. My grandmother lived just one more year after Willa defected, and she didn't like any of the new housekeepers R. B. hired in Willa's place. Neither R. B. nor I knew what to do with this cross, miserable person who had taken the place of my fun-loving grandmother. We wanted the old Daisy to return but she was never coming back, R. B. said, and he made me swear if he got like that, I would put a gun to his head and pull the trigger.

My grandmother didn't utter Willa's name again, but I knew she remembered her because every time we drove past people from the Ipperwash reserve, every time we saw their sad, broken faces, my grandmother would mutter, "I bet they belong to somebody I know."

My grandparents didn't send Willa money after Willa left and they didn't press charges. It was as if Willa hadn't kept my grandmother's house for thirty-one years and helped my grandmother raise her teenage sons and then babysat their childen, one of which happened to be me. I heard from Willa's minister that she'd gone to work for some Free Methodists in Brampton. Willa never spoke or wrote to my grandparents either. Then my grandmother died, and not so long ago, R. B. himself died in a home outside Petrolia.

Yesterday something happened that made me think of them all again. It was the morning rush hour at Spadina station and my twin daughters, Cary and Zoe, were asleep in their strollers, so I was taking the opportunity to read a news clipping that the staff from R. B.'s home had sent on. R. B. had put it in an envelope with my name on it and never mailed it.

Assault Charge

Sixty-five-year-old Willa Jackett of Pembroke Avenue appeared in court on Monday and pleaded not guilty to assaulting Martha Troyer, a wrestling fan, and using obscene language to the annoyance of Miss Troyer.

Acting magistrate Sharon Wilson granted Willa Jackett $200 bail to return for trial January 17. It is alleged that the defendant assaulted Miss Troyer at a Brampton arena for calling the wrestler Bob the Barbarian a midget. Willa Jackett said Miss Troyer had used a derogatory term to refer to people of small stature. Willa Jackett and the wrestler whose name is Robert Hunt are backers of a popular, new Saturday series which features matches with small wrestlers.

I heard the shriek of pneumatic doors and put the clipping back in my purse. I began to push the twins across the platform. Passengers spilled out around me. Cleaning ladies in bright polyester prints, young private school girls in white blouses and tartan skirts, men in shorts carrying briefcases, women tugging at the hands of sleepy-looking children whose high-pitched voices floated above the engine noise.

Then suddenly, in the midst of the crowd, I saw two figures. My grandmother and Willa. My grandmother looked young again and hopeful and she wore a tight-fitting suit the colour of yellow pansies. Willa's hair was braided and she was dressed in her awful white uniform. The two figures stood as if inserted by a child's hand onto the busy platform. Their lifelike stillness was not quite human. But I knew as soon as I saw them standing together, their arms lifted in a frozen wave, that they were saying goodbye.

Dear Cynthia Allerton Cushman

Dear Cynthia:

This is an adult version of "The Stupid Boy Handbook" which I cooked up for your benefit. It's taken me a while because I am a little distracted these days. I have twin girls. My life has changed so much since I last saw you. If only I knew then what I know now,

> *For example:*
> — *I used to think it was impossible to live without a man in my life. Now I see it is only difficult to live without love.*
> — *Once I knew nothing about kiwi fruit or cloth diapers.*

— *There was a time when I thought sex was just lust.*

— *What I once believed was my worst fault— my sensitivity—has turned into my greatest strength.*

— *It amazes me that I ever managed without drawstring garbage bags.*

— *Learning to navigate the shoals of excessive chauvinism is one way girls grow up to be women.*

— *There was a period when I did not like being Canadian.*

— *I am no longer afraid of men's power. The older I get, the more I see the boy in every man, and the woman in me.*

— *All literature is autobiographical, but not in the way many people think.*

— *Size (that is, how tall or short you are) is a metaphysical dimension.*

— *Pepperoni pizzas are not what they used to be.*

By the way, the man I live with is not a stupid boy. In case you wondered I made it through. Write soon, Cynthia, and tell me what happened to you.

The Unabridged Stupid Boy Handbook

Stupid boy glossary

Men — There are still a few around

Guys — Harmless beer drinkers

Dudes — Guys in cowboy boots

Boys — Guys who think they are men

Stupid boys — Guys who think they're hot when they're not

Very Stupid boys — Guys who confuse their ego with their soul

Bad boys — Stupid boys with a philosophy
Love — Something you do with men

Twelve items stupid boys left behind in my apartment

1. A wet towel on my Zen garden.
2. A bag of dirty sportswear in the laundry hamper.
3. Three love poems. By Mussolini.
4. A pregnant husky.
5. A Turkish translation of *Jonathon Livingston Seagull*.
6. A proposal of marriage on the answering machine—in Greek.
7. A guide to lap dancing in Alaska.
8. A broken vibrator, trade name: "The Satisfier." (Its plastic tip melted off because he left it on the radiator.)
9. A basketball.
10. An empty pack of glow-in-the-dark condoms.
11. A red lace bra—not mine. Size 38, D cup.
12. A manual on Tantric sex. Inscribed with a loving message to my best friend.

Stupid boys in the sack

1. Consider foreplay a waste of time.
2. Are better than masturbating—well . . . not really.
3. Pull down their pants and say, "Do you like my purple-helmeted fireman?"
4. Think up "cute" names for your private parts, like "hairy taco."
5. Cover you like wallpaper—constantly.
6. Won't kiss you after you've gone down on them.
7. Save that special moment to say "I love you" when you are sucking their toes—or something.
8. Want you to scream with pleasure even though you're numb by now and bored shitless.
9. Ask—constantly—"Did you come yet?"
10. Stick to the old faithful—missionary monotony.
11. Take their lessons from porn flicks—and only the ones with elevator music.
12. Ask you after they come, "Guess which movie star I look like?"

13. Ask you to go to bed with them and when you say yes, they tell you, "I just wanted to see if you would."
14. Always think sex is better on a water bed.
15. Leave the bathroom door open when they pee so you can continue to admire them.

Sample questionnaire

1. How many stupid boys do you know?
2. How many of them are now politicians?
3. Would you define a stupid boy as:
   a) a guy who doesn't treat you right
   b) an ex-husband
   c) a sloppy kisser
   d) all of the above
4. In your opinion, why are there so many stupid boys in the world? (Please double space your answer to this essay question.)
5. Stupid boys can be feminists. Please discuss.
6. Once a stupid boy, always a stupid boy. True or false?
7. Is your son a stupid boy?

8. Do you think *stupid* is a politically incorrect word? Why or why not?
9. Stupid boys are good to relax with. I mean this in the best possible sense. Why, in your opinion, is this a fair statement?

Please send questionnaire in with stamped and self-addressed envelope. Contributions to any of the above are welcome.

Blessed Immortal Self: How the Jewels Shone on His Skin!

Om namah sivaya, Sankara!

Every day I pray you will attain God and the thrill of holy bliss. (*Om shanti, Sankara!* Or have you forgotten the mantra our master, Vishnu, gave you?)

But you write and say you cannot live without me—that the taste has gone out of your morning tea and a sunset has no beauty because the next day will not have me in it. You say you loved me from the first moment you saw me standing on the ashram dock. You recognized me from Padma's old photographs in our retreat brochure. You said you'd never seen a sweeter yogi than this young woman in the photograph—this brahmacarya with a dark braid down her back doing cartwheels on the beach.

Those pictures were taken more than a dozen years before you stepped off Chandrashekar's ferry with the other guests, still dressed in the clothes of northern cities, as pale and apprehensive as children sent to stay with relatives they didn't know. You said I still looked youthful, leaning over the railing to watch the procession troop ashore, but you were drawn to my mournful eyes. I seemed sad and perplexed for a woman hardly older than your college-girl daughter. And then you noticed how I limped up the path by the yoga platform, lurching slowly past the upside-down bodies of the other guests doing their morning headstands. Behind me trudged Narayan, swearing to himself as he pushed the bamboo cart stacked too high with the suitcases of our guests.

Blessed Immortal Self, you are always polite, but I know you assumed I'd been sleeping with Narayan before you arrived. Believe me, nothing had transpired, although naturally we were thrown together a great deal because our master had asked Narayan and me to prepare his letters for publication. (*Siranda Upanishad*— all the letters are in our master's own handwriting.)

The first day you said you sensed Narayan's possessiveness, but I paid no attention to him or the foolish display he made of himself each morning, chinning himself on the exercise bar in the small courtyard of the ashram. The other women liked to watch the muscles wriggling like snakes in his upper arms. But not me, not your Shakti. Despite his height and physical prowess, to me, Narayan was just a kid with big ears like Jughead in the old Archie comics.

It is true I did enjoy discussing our master with him. Narayan does have a sardonic turn of mind, and he'd visited Swami Vishnu in India, and—oh, Sankara—the amusing stories Narayan can tell about forgetful old gurus meditating in Tibetan caves and getting frostbite because they never come out of their trances! Still, I didn't take Narayan seriously. And that first day, I paid no attention to you either, Sankara. I was carrying Vishnu's forbidden stash of chocolate (which Narayan had just smuggled in), hoping my master wouldn't scold me for being late.

Of course, you had noticed my sprained ankle because you coach basketball like my father, and you've trained yourself to spot an injury. I like to believe our meeting was a necessary form of incest, Sankara (I met you only six months after my father died), but I need to circumvent my nostalgia and tell you the truth. Who else at the Siranda Ashram really worried over my foot? Oh yes, when it didn't heal, some of the staff gave me remedies, but it was only to hear themselves talk. It's ironic, isn't it, that we who serve others often can't serve ourselves.

So it was you who came to my small hut carrying your blue plastic box, the first-aid kit you take everywhere, like a purse under your arm. You found the ice for it in the retreat's failing refrigerator and showed me how to elevate my ankle on pillows and then tape it tightly with a tensor bandage. R.I.C.E.—rest, ice, compression, elevation, you said in a fatherly tone. When the swelling didn't go down, it was you who insisted on taking me to the hospital in the capital.

For that alone, I will always be grateful. But I haven't been fully honest, even here. Because I did notice you the first day. Later in meditation. As you slouched against the whitewashed wall of the temple, not bothering to sit cross-legged like the rest of us, while my master Vishnu chanted his unending *bijas* and mantras. It was the Easter our master grew lax and let those of us with bad backs lean up against the temple wall. So I sat beside you, glad of the chance to rest, and found I couldn't take my eyes off you. What an ugly, ugly old man, I thought. I shivered at the sight of your arms, dappled like chicken skin—your papery hands. You see, there is no point now in hiding how you repulsed me. I even hated the way you'd combed your grey hair into bangs over your forehead. You reminded me of my father during his last month in the hospital. Sankara, he became a mummy the doctor was keeping alive against its wishes. Then you turned to stretch and caught me staring, and I was taken aback by your clear hazel eyes glittering like Krishna's jewels. There's life in the old boy yet, I thought.

Please understand. I do not wish to hurt you. I am trying to be as truthful as I can. So you will understand why I had to go away. You didn't deserve such an unexpected leave-taking, I know. It was several months later. We were old lovers by then and you lay naked in your cabin, your fingers playing with the new black hair on your chest. Once again, you were shaving twice a day and the white hair on your face and chest had started growing in dark. Because of me, you said. Because sex with me was making you young again. Now I am being unfair. You never said "sex." You always said "love." And you weren't greedy about your orgasms. You always pleased me first, as many times as I wanted, and then you pleased yourself.

Seven for me and one for you. That way we're even, you said. No man has ever been so easy or gracious with me. Too often lovers want to please a woman out of anxiety or vanity. Not for the thrill of it, not like you.

That day, our last day together, I felt happy as I dipped my hands in a bowl of milk. I was cleaning the altar beads, made of real rudraska, the expensive wood my guru admired. I remember letting the beads spill into my palm. They were still damp, not sticky the way sandalwood gets if you clean it in milk.

I sat down on the bed beside you and with one hand began to stroke your forehead. I knew every inch of you by then, Sankara, and yet I still struggled to overcome my dread when you reached out for me. And then, when I touched you, I wondered why I had to struggle. I loved the feel of your skin. It wasn't dry the way I imagined an old man's skin would be. It was slightly oily and surprisingly pliant. Wait. I lie again. Your body felt soft, like foreskin.

As I began to place the slippery beads on your body, I noticed Narayan doing his chin-ups in the courtyard outside your window. He couldn't see me at first. How could he see in the glare of the morning sun? It turned everything except the roiling green ocean a sulphureous yellow. He seemed to be looking for someone. Then he swung down and heaved his knapsack onto his shoulders and walked over to your hut. Then just as I was putting the first two beads on the lids of your closed eyes, he whistled. Very softly, he moved the shutter ajar. I looked up and he beckoned.

Frightened, I poured a bunch of beads into one of your ears whose drooping lobes I liked to nibble. My clumsiness made you giggle.

My hand trembling, I took the beads from your ear and began to place them deep in all the silky crevices of your sun-baked body. You were lightly brown by then, like tulasi wood. I lined up four, maybe five, in the creases on either side of your groin where the skin was very pale.

Blessed Immortal Self, how the jewels shone on your skin! You looked beautiful and I was glad the spy at our window could see you, splendid in my master's jewellery.

You accepted my little game, eyes closed, smiling, like Krishna in his portrait on the temple altar. You know the picture I mean—the one my master Vishnu has me drape with beads, like the wreaths our families still hang on Christmas trees . . . the very same beads I was putting on you that morning, our last time together.

I smiled back down at you and you started to run your narrow tongue over your lips, as if already you could taste me.

With my still-shaking hand, I took the biggest jewel, the 109th bead that tells us when we've come to the end of a mantra, and I touched it to the tip of your penis. Instantly, your penis swung upward, erect again, and your glittering hazel eyes flew open, but you couldn't see Narayan who stood silently watching us at the window. I placed the bead in the sunken hole of your belly button, where it nested like one of my master's unblinking eyes.

Sighing, you stroked my cheek.

"Sit astride me, Shakti."

"Yes," I whispered.

You see, my dearest, you weren't the only one who thought I made you young. Each time you penetrated me—stroke by stroke, slowly at first and then faster and slowly again, ah, Sankara, how I like those slow strokes—each time you pushed into me, you lost some of your seventy-one years! And by the time our lovemaking was done, you were young again, even younger than me. Yes, each time we had sex I rescued from death the Methuselah I'd noticed on the first day.

That morning, knowing Narayan watched us, I wanted to please you and show the doubting Narayan that you were as virile as a young man in the bedroom. So I crouched down, excited by Narayan's jealousy, and prepared myself to summon up in you all your gorgeous youth. Let Narayan feast his eyes upon us! He had a lesson or two ahead of him! The arrogant boy!

Something made me look again at the window. You were still too absorbed to notice, but there, peeking around the shutter, was Narayan's face. I stared proudly back into his wondering eyes and saw the shock and disgust I'd often felt before I touched you—the feelings I anxiously pushed aside and said nothing about, not to you or anyone because I was too ashamed.

I stopped our lovemaking and stood up. I was trembling.

"What's wrong, sweetheart?" you asked.

"I don't know," I said.

In a panic, I fled to my cabin to think. You see, that morning, in Narayan's eyes, I saw not only you, Sankara, as you lay before me, bedecked in my master's beads, but myself. Why was I with a man so many years my senior? Why did I promise I would never leave you when you plucked at me with your greedy fingers?

Was it vanity that kept me by your side? Because I made your white hair grow in dark, did I think you needed me to keep you young? Yes, that is how I felt, Sankara, and it angered me that you didn't understand what you asked. You always told me not to worry—that age is only the accumulation of numbers, and has nothing to do with the heart. But loving you had become a burden, and I resented you for being old.

I knew I had to make a choice. I could be with you or be with a man like Narayan who wouldn't exact your price but lacked the wisdom to love with full acceptance.

And so, my beloved, I live now with Narayan in——a new spiritual community Vishnu, our master, has started near the capital of——. My guru forwards your letters to me, and I read them with great sorrow. Narayan says if you loved me, you would release me and not write begging for my return. He says you are a vampire who doesn't have my real interests at heart. Narayan is young and doesn't choose words judiciously, but in one respect he is right. I gave you back what I could of your youth. Now it is my turn to have the gift bestowed on me. Farewell, Sankara! You who loved me the way nobody else has. Without limits or judgement. You'd never seen anyone so supple, you said, as this young woman in Padma's photographs. You admired her bare legs bending backwards into a human wheel.

Thine own Shakti

Interim Pleasures

MY HUSBAND, David, said Harper drove his motorcycle like a psychic wedge through our home, picking up our old antique pine desk, our green felt love seat and stained-glass windows, and dragging them off like booty behind his huge Kawasaki bike. My husband said Harper didn't notice what he'd done because he was already restless after two days in our home, restless and impatient to get on the road again like the Marlboro cowboy. The Marlboro cowboy with black skin because Harper was an African-American. He was the last of my boyfriends, the only one who hadn't given David and me his blessing. David had met the others—I called them party boys because they belonged to a time in my life when I didn't want anybody serious around. I was looking for a little distraction, which was a whole lot easier to find than most women imagine.

But Harper had stayed out of sight. Harper remained a voice on the telephone, a silky male voice calling at strange hours like 7:00 a.m., as if I was still available. Often Harper called before or after my lovemaking with David as if he was already in the bedroom with us, a tall restless presence in a worn leather jacket waiting for the right moment to butt in.

That's my husband David's story anyway. And it's true Harper did cause problems. There's never been any doubt about that. I am a writer and my name is Kirby Johansson. Before I married David and moved to Toronto, I lived in New York's West Village and spent my summers teaching English at an American college in Athens. It was a sweet situation for a while, I can tell you, although I don't want to go on too much about my past. I am the first to admit that romance has its jagged side. But as soon as you realize rejection isn't going to kill you (it just doesn't feel good), any woman can have the time of her life. I'm serious. We all need time out. The secret is to pick men who, like you, are eager to experience the pleasures of intermission.

interval *noun* 1. intervening time or space; pause. 2. break, gap, especially in theatre. 3. (Music) difference of pitch between two sounds, in melody or harmony. 4. distance between persons or things in respect of qualities. *See* interim, intermission, rest period, caesura, interruption, hiatus, etc.

In the summer of 1990, I met Harper at the Taconda Writers' Workshop. I'd been travelling hard across Europe and the Mediterranean and I landed in the Green Mountains of Vermont in my tie-dyed Turkish sundress, listening to Leonard Cohen sing "First We Take Manhattan" on my Sony Walkman.

As far as I was concerned, Harper was a man for the interregnum. I recognized the signs when he came towards me on the second day, wearing a motorcycle helmet with a clear plastic full-face visor, his huge hands in black leather gloves. The flirtatious smile. The easy disregard for the timid-looking woman with a ponytail sitting on his bike watching us. She was the woman I'd noticed bringing him breakfast in the old camp dining hall. All the writers at my table and myself had watched her shyly sweet-talk one of the waiters into getting freshly scrambled eggs for Harper. The eggs had run out by the time we sat down, and we were eating cereal and the thick, brackish liquid known at Taconda as Yankee coffee. The woman with a ponytail had passed our table holding the plate of fresh eggs for Harper like she was a page holding a pillow with the king's crown. Somebody had said she was married, but that didn't stop her from following Harper around like a lost dog.

I wanted to warn her.

I wanted to tell her she had to beware—not of Harper, but of herself. Of her own vanity, and the unfounded optimism that makes a woman think she can bag an interim man. Interim men aren't interested in something permanent. The role of somebody like Harper is to get you interested—to be the perfect possibility you may one day take.

party *noun and verb* **1**. social gathering, usually of invited guests. **2**. body of persons engaged in an activity or travelling together. **3**. group of people united in a cause. **4**. person forming one side of an agreement or dispute. **5**. accessory to an action. **6**. person (colloquial). *See* fun, good-time, conviviality, jollity, merry-making, heartiness, cheer, the glad hand, etc.

I avoided Harper. When he started sending me looks across the lecture hall, I studied my notes. And I passed by without a glance when I saw the crowd of women taking his picture during lunch hour. Harper wrote travel books and he liked having his picture taken beside his motorcycle. He stood with his arms crossed under a Vermont pine tree, looking lanky and mean—just the way he posed on the jacket of his books. Out of the corner of my eye, I'd catch him sneaking looks at me, pretending to be indifferent to his giggling fans. I used to feel a little sorry for Harper then. He was trying so hard to please. But I didn't respond. I knew he had to get on about his business. All writers have personas to contend with and Harper's persona was catnip for women. Harper wrote on behalf of the thousands of African-Americans who couldn't speak for themselves.

Just picking up his laptop was a bigger responsibility for Harper than for most of us.

Of course, Harper made his way to me. He would. In the small cabin, where the staff went to drink after the workshops, he accused me of avoiding him, of dodging his offers to play tennis. He said he'd seen me on the courts behind the barn, playing with some of the other writers when the workshops ended. Why wouldn't I play with him?

"Maybe next week," I said. "Besides, you look like you have your hands full."

"What are you talking about?" Harper said. "I sleep alone every night. It's pathetic."

"Sure you do," I laughed. I'd seen not only the timid woman with a ponytail but clusters of East Coast college girls crowding into Harper's class. He taught with Wiley Smith, the famous ex-editor of the *Atlantic Monthly* and their workshop was packed with women of all ages and skin colour. Every morning, on the way to my own work-shop, I saw them jostling each other for the best seats. That is, the seats close to the front where Harper paced back and forth. Wiley was at least seventy-two, and he sat behind a desk and let Harper do the class.

"You're one of the only people here I can talk to," Harper said. "You and Wiley Smith."

Either you're lying, I thought, or you're the smartest man I've ever met. And all right, even then I knew— Harper wasn't lying.

We played tennis every day after that on the graceful sprawling clay courts, the courts that Robert Frost and

John Gardner had once played on at Taconda, and every day Harper beat me. He'd learned to play tennis by watching TV because his parents thought the sport was a waste of time and wouldn't pay for lessons. But his childhood hadn't been as difficult as you might think, Harper said. He grew up on Long Island, the son of a car salesman. His mother was an operator for a telephone company and he'd gone to a private boys' school. He was the one black face among all the white boys and they treated him well. He'd gone on a scholarship. Scholarships pretty well kept him going right through college; he even went to the Iowa Writers' Workshop on a scholarship deal. And now he taught there when he needed the money.

There was a problem, however. I met Harper when I began to tire of romance.

romance *noun and verb intransitive* **1.** *cap* (Romish) vernacular language (or pertaining to language) of old France, Italy, Spain, Provence, etc. (collect.) the languages descended from Latin. **2.** an old word for story. **3.** prose or verse tale with incidents remote from everyday life. **4.** an exaggeration, (a) picturesque falsehood.

See (*verb*) play the fool, blunder, talk nonsense, frisk, caper, play practical jokes, etc.

For the first time in my life, I was considering love. I thought I was overdue. I'd been married briefly in my early twenties so I knew living with somebody was a Zen discipline that demanded patience and devotion. I preferred romantic interludes. I didn't like middles, I liked beginnings. And, as I said, I realized I could survive the end when either you dropped them, or they dropped you, but it didn't matter much because you both knew it wasn't going to last anyhow. It was always best just to cut your losses and move on.

Knowing this, I am surprised I let somebody like Harper get to me. I felt it start after our first tennis game. Harper's power over me. We lay under the pines on the grass beside the court and I punched him on the stomach for beating me and he laughed and put his arm around my shoulders. The woman with a ponytail was nowhere to be seen. Only a few girls watched us from the veranda of one of the workshop cabins. I could feel their envy a mile off but they had cheered every time I won a point and they had booed when Harper beat me. These girls were writer wannabes who took waitressing positions in the dining room until they published their own books and could come back as teachers themselves. Mid-list authors such as Harper and me weren't as intimidating as writers like the celebrity poet at Taconda whose novel in verse had been on the *New York Times* bestseller list for 109 weeks. Harper's publisher and mine didn't print 100,000 copies of our books, or send us out on a twenty-six city tour, but they published us because our books got reviewed, and sometimes reprinted.

I waved back at them and Harper laughed. Two weeks later, at the closing dance, they pinned a white carnation on Harper and I ate it off his lapel as they danced around us, clapping and shrieking. This was the final night of the workshop, which had turned out to be a month spent with Harper playing tennis and volleyball and hiking to the founder's cabin a few miles from campus. On the last morning, I brought Harper freshly scrambled eggs, just the way I'd seen the woman with a pony tail do on the first day.

I told my husband I admired Harper for what he'd accomplished. David likes accomplished people. He is from a Jewish family in Buenos Aires. He is fifteen years older than me, a stocky, nice-looking man with a reddish beard who worries he might lose me to someone younger and more fit. He blames his preoccupation with rivals on his Latin background. Neither David's age nor weight has ever bothered me. I like heavy-set men because I am a big woman myself. I stand five foot nine in my stocking feet and I weigh 175 pounds.

In North American literary circles, David is known for his anthologies of Latin American fiction. He also produces educational documentaries for a Toronto television station.

"You'll like Harper when you meet him," I told David. "But just remember — Harper's a rolling stone."

By that, I meant David had no reason to worry. I wasn't interested in a man like Harper any more. Harper avoided relationships. David listened without saying anything.

David says there are too many gaps in my story about Harper. There are no gaps, I tell him. We lived together for only a few weeks in the West Village. And I saw Harper just once or twice after that. I can't remember much sex, I tell David. Mostly, I remember Harper getting on his motorcycle. I would stand by the curb, and hand Harper his astronaut-like helmet, and Harper would put it on with a regretful shake of his head. "Time to play road warrior again," he'd say. And then he was off without a backward glance. The last time it happened, I didn't want to play my part. I didn't want to be the handmaiden offering the helmet, the gloves and the goodbye kiss. And the longing. Harper always wanted my longing. He needed it to keep him warm when he was far from home. Harper had no fixed address so I sent postcards to his parents' house, and just when I thought he had forgotten all about me, he would call from halfway around the world and say he missed me. He saved his affectionate words for the end of the phone call, the moment before he hung up.

I didn't tell Harper how I cried when I saw his back disappearing down the road. Or how I longed for him when he was gone. Or how, the night before he left, I'd start to fret over the distance that he was going to put between us. Even before Harper set off, I already pictured him on his Kawasaki, a hooded figure crouched behind his windscreen—a bullet man cracking through New England hills and meadows, arcing over Georgia swamps and Midwestern plains—flowing like the wind across America—the towns and cities rolling by— Lynchburg, Lynn, Luverne, Lund, Lava Beds—Harper, the human-hurricane leaving me behind—Couchfield, Chatham, Chelmsford, Cambridge, Cranford, Coventry, Chester, Carlisle—Harper, going, going, gone— Kovel, Kishinev, Kherson, Kremenchuk, Kharkov, Kursk, Kozlov, Kolomna, Kiev . . .

Where exactly is the point when you know a person has left you, I wondered? Was Harper gone the moment he turned his bike up Sixth Avenue, and I could no longer see him? Or did the point depend on sound? Maybe Harper went out of my life when he was no longer within calling distance.

Harper is only one foot away, I'd tell myself when he sat down beside me to watch Letterman. When Harper went into the bathroom to wash his socks, I'd count ten—ah—twelve and a half feet.

Once by accident, fifteen minutes after Harper had left me, I was driving in a friend's car on Houston Street. "Isn't that your guy?" my friend said. She pointed to a tall, helmeted figure at a gaseteria. It was Harper, filling his bike. I shook my head. It didn't matter. As far as I was concerned, Harper was as good as gone.

I didn't tell Harper how much I missed him. I didn't tell him about my counting game. I always left that out. And I didn't tell David about it either.

The last time Harper called I was in England. David spoke to him, and when Harper said he was passing through Toronto, David invited him to stay. "I think it's time I met this phantom in person," David told me when I returned. David had heard of cases back in Argentina where old lovers could extract more loyalty than a partner because over time the fantasy we construct gets severed from the memory of the person. Eventually, David said, the fantasy even supplants the memory itself.

"I don't want to live with someone whose first fantasy is not me," David told me. "Would you?"

"Oh, don't be such a worry wart," I said. "I was over Harper ages ago."

Two weeks later, Harper phoned again and said he was coming the following week.

gap *noun* **1**. unfilled space or interval. **2**. breach in a hedge or wall. **3**. wide divergence in views. **4**. gorge or pass; i.e., fill or close a gap, making up a deficiency. **Gap-toothed** *adjective*, having gaps between the teeth. *See* gapped, gappy.

In our large green Toronto dining room, Harper is talking about violence. He has to fight, he says. Because white men like to test themselves against a black man his size. David's sitting across from Harper, listening sympathetically. Harper's sitting beside me. It's an early July day—a day of detente and renewal. President Clinton is restoring diplomatic rights with Vietnam and the Pope has just apologized for his church's part in holding back the cause of women. I am aware of David's nervous generosity. But I am bone-weary from teaching a writing workshop at the university. I want to go to bed and stop pretending I am glad to see Harper when I am shocked to find him taking his ease in my home. Shocked to see his shapely black hands eating the shrimp penne David made in Harper's honour. And shocked that David is sitting there, the amiable host, letting Harper bait him about his size and his colour.

"Oh, come on, Harper. When was your last fight?" I ask crossly.

"About twenty years ago," Harper winks and laughs, and I can't help laughing either.

David smiles anxiously.

After we go to bed, David and I do not make love.

Two days before Harper arrived, David told me he'd dreamt about a battered Kawasaki bike outside our house. The phantom lover was here. Harper had arrived. David climbed our steps, he called out, no one answered. Then he saw the worn leather jacket hanging on the bannister. There's something about a black leather jacket. Especially a jacket whose leather fringe is eaten away, as if a band of tough moths had worked it over. Nervously, David climbed a second set of stairs to the bedrooms. The door of the guest bedroom was closed. He called out again. No answer. He opened the door a crack and there we were—me astride Harper's lanky black body, my head tilted back in a trance. David hurried down to the kitchen and poured himself a Jameson. He jumped a litttle when we came to find him. Harper didn't apologize. He just walked over and shook David's hand. Then Harper steered me out the door.

Poor David. Now I can sympathize.

But it didn't go like that exactly. On the first day of Harper's visit, I found David bringing Harper coffee.

"Look who's here!" David kissed me. "Isn't it wonderful to see Harper?"

Harper sat sprawled on our loveseat. He looked too comfortable to move.

"What a surprise!" I said grumpily.

David thrust a paperback into my hand.

"Look, Kirby. Your friend has written a travel book on Japan!"

"Yeah."

"I think I can use it on my show."

I scowled. "Oh, great."

"Hey, Kirby!" Harper laughed. "You jealous I'm going to be on TV?"

"Who says I'm not going to be on TV too?"

David looked doubtful.

"Well, not on this show," David said.

The next day Harper accompanied me to my workshop. He talked sincerely and openly about the life of a travel writer and what it meant to be black. My students wrote down the names of his books.

Watch out, Kirby, I thought, as we walked home together across the campus. Harper's starting to get to you.

The morning was very humid. Small, frothy balls of moisture clung to the spruce near the Gothic clock tower. Even Harper, who had biked twice across the Australian desert, felt the heat. At the gates of the university, Harper stopped. He put his gloved hand on my shoulder.

"Kirby, did I do okay?"

"Do okay?" My voice trembled. "You were great!"

Harper grinned.

When we got home, I hurried into the kitchen to make Harper lunch. He was going to visit David at the television station. Maybe it wasn't so bad having Harper stay with us. At least David would get the chance to see that somebody like Harper wasn't a threat. And the two men seemed to like each other. David and Harper. Harper and David. It's ring sounded better than Kirby and Harper. Harper and Kirby. Which is what Harper once told me everybody said. Our names were irretrievably joined when people spoke of the Vermont workshop. We were considered inseparable, Harper had written. The duo of the year.

In the kitchen, I helped Harper to two bowls of David's shrimp penne.

"Did David really read to Borges when he was a kid?" Harper asked.

"Yes. Before he got messed up with politics."

"Is that why he had to leave Argentina?"

I nodded. "He used to teach the tango in Toronto until he got his job in television."

"The tango, huh?" Harper wrinkled his nose.

"David's a *porteño*, a man from Buenos Aires. They take the tango seriously there. It's not the dance we know. The men used to do it together in the brothels."

I executed a few steps—*slow slow, quick quick, slow*.

Harper stopped eating and looked at his watch.

"Cool—very cool," he said and grabbed his leather jacket and left.

love *noun and verb* **1**. hold dear, bear love to, be in love with; *love me, love my dog,* or *Lord love you!* (exclamation of surprise). **2**. formula in game of forfeits; (love-forty, tennis). **3**. cling to, delight in, enjoy having, be addicted to, admire or be glad of the existence of (love life, honour, comfort, golf, etc.). *See* desire, affection, partiality, wish for, hankering, liking, be bent upon, crave, pine for, hope, etc.

That night Harper and David called me from a downtown bistro.

"Come join us," David said. "I'm taking Harper out on the company."

When I arrived, David was slouched against a wall bench, finishing a story about Borges convincing his young female companion to wash his underwear. It was a Borges story I hated. Both men stopped laughing as I sat down.

"You never told me his next book is going to be on Latin America," David said, slurring "his."

"Is that true, Harper?"

"Uh-huh." Harper smiled at David and David smiled back.

"Really?" I sat down and scanned the menu and David pushed across his plate of half-eaten swordfish.

"Finish this. Harper wants to see a Latin club. So I thought we'd go to Cuba Libre."

"But you hate its drag show!" I glared at David and Harper grinned.

He drummed his fingers on the table. "Kirby, I've got to start my book somewhere."

I ate David's swordfish and then we left the restaurant and got into David's car. David opened the door to the back seat for me.

"Harper needs the extra leg room," David said.

Harper slipped into the front seat beside David. I got in the back. I was still very tired, even more tired than I had been the night before, and I wished David would just shut up about Harper moving to Canada. But

David kept yakking on about the advantages of living outside the United States. How glad he was he'd left Argentina and come to Canada. How he liked Canadian civility; how he even liked Toronto and its winters. To the south—could Harper see it—was the SkyDome, the largest sports centre in the world with a retractable roof, and over there—that hypodermic needle was the CN Tower—the tallest free-standing structure in the world.

I didn't look at the landmarks. I kept my eyes on Harper's dark angular head which inclined this way or that, depending on where David told him to look.

"Harper, did you have a good day?" I asked.

"Harper had a wonderful day," David said. "We talked about his book for two hours in my office and then we went out and discussed it some more."

I frowned. I wanted to stretch but Harper was in the front seat, taking up all the room.

"I've got the go-ahead. I can put Harper in my documentary on Japan," David said. "Reading from his wonderful new book."

"How nice for you."

Harper turned around and faced me.

"Kirby—" he said. "David's cool."

"Yes," I said. "Yes, I guess he is."

After David read the passionate welcome note I'd left for Harper on the first afternoon, a love declaration if ever David saw one, David knew—well, he knew that I still loved Harper. No wonder David dreamed about coming home and discovering me astride Harper. It took Harper to set him right. Harper—the truth-teller, the man's man. No wonder David kept talking about Harper moving to Toronto. About the film they were going to do together. About the new bands from Africa and the fetish clubs David wanted to show Harper if Harper would only stay longer.

On his way to the club, Harper wanted to stop at a doughnut shop. As soon as Harper was out of sight, David turned towards me.

"You don't understand Harper."

"What are you talking about?"

"You know very well what I am talking about," David said. "Harper told me he never had any romantic feelings about you. It was all in your head."

"Harper told you this?" I reached for one of David's cigarettes. The thought of Harper not liking sex with me made me want to put something in my mouth.

"And that's not all," David said. "Harper told me

he would never tolerate his girlfriend having an old boyfriend over."

"Harper has a girlfriend?"

"Of course he does," David said. "Somebody he met at that writers' workshop you went to."

"Yeah. And now he's attracted to you," I snapped. "You're just drunk."

"I'm not drunk." David sighed. "You women. Sometimes you don't understand us, that's all."

I watched Harper walking back from the doughnut shop. He held the brown grease-spotted bag under his arm like a football. And when he saw David, he smiled and pitched it through David's window. David caught it and Harper laughed, and David laughed too. Harper didn't look back at me as he opened the car door. Instead he sat down with a sigh as if it was a relief to park his big body in the front seat beside my husband. I could feel myself get quiet. What if I did have Harper wrong? Maybe he'd only been humouring me when we had sex. Maybe he'd been trying to tell me this all along.

David reached over and patted Harper's knee.

"Ready for Cuba Libre?" David said.

"Ready, boss," Harper said.

brotherhood *noun* **1.** relationship (as) between brothers; companionship. **2.** association, society, or community of people linked by a common interest. **3.** trade union. **4.** community of feeling between all human beings. *See* similarity, family likeness, fraternity, intimacy, intercourse, fellowhood.

It was eleven o'clock when I dragged myself up the stairs to Cuba Libre. Harper went first, then David, then me. The new order.

At the bar, David ordered Jameson for himself and Harper. I asked the bartender for a peach schnapps. Harper sat between us on a leather couch facing the mirrored octagonal room.

On the dance floor, the drag show was just ending. Two queens, both in white satin and enormous plumed white-feathered headdresses, were doing the tango to "La Jalousie." The song was once a favourite of mine. I first heard it at Waldo's, where David taught ballroom dancing. I started to hum.

David smiled at Harper.

"I'm tired but Kirby is getting ready to whoop it up," he said. "Do you mind doing the honours?"

"I'm tired too," Harper sighed.

"Forget it, Harper," I said.

"She thinks I will be upset if she dances with you." David signalled to the waiter for more scotch. "Well, that's silly. I don't mind. I should let her have some time alone with you." David leaned across Harper and winked stagily. "Kirby, just don't keep Harper on his feet very long. He has to get up early tomorrow."

"David, please," I said.

"Hey, Kirby—how about it?" Harper stood up and held out his arms.

"Go on, Kirby. Don't make our guest dance by himself," David said and gave me a little push.

"David, I have to talk to you." I stood up and waited and finally David stood up too, shrugging at Harper as he took me in his arms. Harper sat back down on the couch.

The DJ put on "La Cumparsita," another tango song, and the drag queens were now pulling people out of the audience. In one long slow movement everyone sitting on chairs was gradually getting on their feet and starting to dance again.

"Did Harper really tell you he had no romantic feelings for me?" I said as soon as we were out of earshot.

David didn't answer. He was looking at something over my shoulder.

"David, why do you believe Harper and not me?"

"Kirby, over there!" David tilted his chin. "Poor Harper!"

Harper was standing in the middle of the floor, listening to one of the drag queens. She was trying to show Harper the number eight, a step that requires the woman to sit on the man's crossed legs.

David groaned. "The tango is sober, melancholy! It's not that nonsense the Germans do."

"David, are you listening?"

He was already lurching over to Harper.

David bowed a little unsteadily.

"Let me show you how it's done!"

Before Harper could answer, David spun him out into the centre of the floor, holding Harper in the classic pose: left arm around Harper's waist, his right arm clasping Harper's. *Slow slow, quick quick, slow.* David was stumbling slightly but Harper didn't seem to mind. He was nodding and listening closely to what David was saying. And then all at once Harper's hips started to float beneath him and he began taking long, gliding steps.

Harper was doing the tango the way it was meant to be done: his head haughtily forward, looking away from

David—Harper's upper body stiff as his legs furiously curled and uncurled in tandem with David's. How could Harper master the steps so quickly? He had learned to play tennis by watching television. Harper was a natural athlete.

A drag queen plucked at my arm.

"You, girl! Don't be shy!" She smelled of Pour Monsieur, a cologne David liked to buy.

"Sprained ankle." I pointed at my foot and walked out, limping.

brothel *noun* 1. house where prostitution takes place. (originally *brothel-house* from Old English *breothan* go to ruin, and Middle English *brothel* worthless man)

I walked along the hilly boulevard outside the club, past the Portuguese shops and travel agencies, and along a quiet street where red and white rose bushes trellised up the terraced houses. And as I walked, I cried and cursed myself for loving David. I felt as if all the men I'd ever been close with had disappointed me. And I hated myself for needing such undeveloped creatures who could behave outrageously and still claim my affection. I'd been full of hope and goodwill when

David and I took our vows, but my faith in what we were doing had started to waver the afternoon Harper showed up.

It wasn't even love I felt for Harper. I felt envy. I'd admired the ease with which he fled from me and the messy, sometimes suffocating pleasures a life together offered. I'd wanted to be like Harper, riding away from all ties and obligations, with only the promise of the road ahead.

I stopped. Down by the Chinese theatre, a police car had started up and was crawling in my direction, its siren light winking, but making no sound. The cruiser drove slowly by some Portuguese boys sitting on the hood of a nearby car, eating ice cream. Then it inched past me, its headlights sweeping my dress, while the cop looked me up and down. I pretended I didn't hear it pull up to the curb and the whine of a car window going down. I hurried down the street to the Cuba Libre and went inside.

Upstairs, David was sitting by himself on the couch.

"Kirby, I thought you'd left!" He jumped up and offered me his seat.

"Where's your friend?" I said maliciously.

David pointed drunkenly at a space near one of the

mirrored walls. At first, I couldn't see anything under the flash of the strobe. Then I spotted a man in a sleeveless vest dancing by himself. Harper, the fool. I stared in astonishment. Harper was watching his reflection. He looked beautiful. Every so often a woman appeared beside Harper and gyrated hopefully. Harper didn't notice. He couldn't take his eyes off the dark god in the glass, pulsing, always just out of reach.

Eighteen—seventeen and a half—fourteen—now thirteen and a half . . . From across the dance floor, Harper saw me. He waved and began to spin clownishly round and round for my benefit.

David groaned.

"Kirby, I wish I'd never asked him here."

"It's okay, David." I took his hand.

"You sure?"

I nodded.

Ten—yes, five—three.

Harper weaved over and the three of us went home.

The next morning, before David left for work, he said Harper was downstairs waiting for me.

Sure enough, Harper was slumped on my velvet love seat. His motorcycle jacket rested across his thigh.

An omen of the leave-taking to come. He stood up.

"Sorry about last night. David and I were pretty pissed."

"Did you really never have romantic feelings about me, Harper?"

"Kirby, I got to hit the road."

"Look. I was never serious about you either," I said. "But you didn't have to lie like that!"

"You were never serious about me?" Harper asked. "Is that because I'm black?"

"Don't be stupid. You were never around long enough."

"You sure it's not a racial thing?"

"Has anyone told you, you can be a real asshole?"

Harper grinned. "Do you know where my helmet is?"

"Here." I picked Harper's helmet up off the hall table and handed it over. He took it and put his long arms around me.

"Did David tell you I'm seeing someone?"

"Somebody from Taconda, I hear."

"From Iowa," Harper said. "A creative writing prof. She reminds me of you."

Harper kissed me on the lips. I just stood there.

Two inches—or so.

"I'm sure going to miss you," Harper sighed.

Harper lowered his helmet over his head and kissed me again with a little more pressure. I smiled. One foot, spot on. Then he yanked down the face visor and put on his jacket. Harper started going down the stairs—five, six, seven, thirteen—I watched his broad leather back go out my door—fifteen—the door slammed—twenty, twenty-five, thirty—I heard the Kawasaki start up—two hundred—the roar of his bike resounded like thunder up and down the street—then I heard it growing fainter—five hundred—eight hundred—what did it matter? He was gone.

A few years later, David brought home Harper's book on Latin America. We read the quotes on its back cover together. A celebrated travel writer had called Harper's account of the the southern hemisphere "the travel book of the decade." Another reviewer from a newsmagazine said Harper's prose was "a triumph of fact and fiction." In the jacket photograph, Harper stood in the middle of an Iowa cornfield. He'd grown a beard and his eyes looked a little weary, but he was still Harper, the man for the interregnum, standing with his arms crossed over his big leathered chest.

Yes, it was Harper all right, ready and waiting for what the world has in store, the perfect possibility, just as I remembered him.

Christmas Day at the Yoga Camp

ALL MORNING Dix knew something bad was about to happen. She felt it in the perplexing humidity which had kept Emma's underpants from drying on the clothesline for three days and in the oily presence of the ocean hitting the shore by her feet. She saw it in the western sky behind the lighthouse, beyond the sandbar where Emma was swimming, beyond the anchored yachts, beyond even the tiny body of a parasailor floating, curled from the parachute harness like a small silkworm, spinning a little and drifting on its own thread. Not there, but out, way out to the horizon where a ridge of darkening mauve cloud hung like a backdrop for the dreadful thing Dix felt coming. Maybe the reason for

Dix's distress lay far out there too, out beyond the coral reefs, in the zone of ocean traffic where Dix saw a clumsy old ship with sails like an Arab dhow. The old ship appeared to be sailing right out of the low-lying purple storm clouds. Dix lifted her binoculars up for a closer look, and sure enough the deck of the old boat was jammed to the brim with tiny perishable bodies, all with heads and faces darker than hers or Emma's, and the faces appeared to be looking at Dix sitting on a beach chair in her yellow bikini.

Or perhaps they were looking at the yoga campers who stood on the wooden platform behind Dix, their arms stretched towards the sun. Above the platform, in bright tropical colours, somebody had painted the high, domed forehead and elephantine ears of the late Swami Sevada, who had founded the Sevada Yoga Retreat. There were dozens of these hand-painted signs all over the ashram—signs advocating proper rest, diet, exercise and relaxation, signs with the sad, fleshy face of Swami Sevada recommending the joys of selfless service, or arrow-shaped signs pointing to the numerous small meditation glades on the property which had once belonged to a real English lady.

Dix doubted that the Sevada Yoga Retreat would be the first thing any refugee would choose to see. It was

Dix's first Christmas alone with Emma since the divorce and she'd come to the ashram for solace. But if Dix was a refugee, she wouldn't want her boat to beach itself in front of an ashram which asked its guests to sign pledges promising not to drink coffee or alcohol, not to smoke or eat garlic, onions, meat or fish, not to sunbathe nude, and last of all, not to ask for refunds.

Dix knew the refugees were from Haiti because two days before, she'd asked Sarasvati, the British swami, about another boat like this one, and Sarasvati had shaken her head and said the boat came from Haiti and had no chance of landing. The Bahamians didn't like the Haitians, Sarasvati said, because they bred like rabbits, hoping they'd be allowed to stay if their children were born in the Bahamas. Sarasvati stood on the platform behind Dix now, her instructions to the yoga class booming out through the sound system, along with the snuffly, squeaking noises of the wind getting picked up on the amp.

Sarasvati sounded tired. Yesterday, they had run out of water because it was Christmas and there were too many people for the facilities, so the campers had to bring seawater in buckets to prime the johns. Sarasvati called their bucket brigades "doing karma yoga," and she had smiled at Dix who had gone back down for another bucket, and then another, after many of the guests had given up.

Afterwards, Sarasvati seemed grateful and she'd taken Dix to the Health Hut where the two women talked about Sarasvati's decision to accept the vow of celibacy. The late Swami Sevada had encouraged them to give sex up slowly, Sarasvati giggled, and that's what she did. But their organization had no patience for the ones who kept having affairs. Recently, a young French-Canadian had been banished for falling in love with the tennis pro from Club Med. The Sevada Retreat was a serious ashram, Sarasvati said. You could bend the rules, but you couldn't break them openly.

Dix felt pleased that Sarasvati had confided in her. The older woman was known for being standoffish and Dix wished Roger, her ex-husband, could see her enjoying the company of a diffident, middle-aged swami. The thought had made Dix laugh, and for a moment she forgot how lonely she felt without Roger.

Dix longed to get to know Sarasvati better, and she sensed the older woman felt the same way about Dix but her position as head of the crowded camp made it difficult. Before meals, when the campers lined up at the food tables, Dix would look around for Sarasvati, and she'd smile at her and the older woman would smile back. The swami always sat with the enormously fat camp gardener, and Sarasvati looked pleased but slightly distant when Dix and Emma walked by and spoke to her. Sarasvati didn't invite Dix to join them.

Once or twice, in the morning, after meditation, the swami had asked Dix to pass around the bowl of nuts and dried fruits, and Dix knew this was a sign she was favoured. She longed to take Sarasvati aside and tell her how frightened she felt on her own, but the dream had made Dix self-conscious.

The night after the bucket brigade, Dix had dreamt about Sarasvati's breast. The dream was strangely horrible because the swami's breast had been severed from her body. And right before Dix's eyes, the breast grew as long and pointy as the cone-shaped homes of African termite colonies whose pictures Dix used to see in *National Geographic* when she was Emma's age. Even worse: in the dream, Dix lay on the sand, trussed up with red Christmas bows, while a troop of young Hindu monks rolled the weird, discarnate breast up the beach towards her. The monks were huffing and puffing and giggling like Emma when she said the word "poop," and their shaved heads reached only halfway up the side of the gigantic breast whose colour, now that Dix thought about it, was the same shade of elephant grey as the trunks of the royal palms at the Sevada Yoga Retreat. One last detail. When the delicate skin of the breast touched Dix, its nipple began to spout milk and Dix burst out singing "Let it Snow."

Beyond the string of bobbing orange buoys, a dog was barking and a yellow dinghy was being lowered from one of the anchored yachts. Two figures scrambled down into it, and one of the figures began to row, spinning the yellow raft crazily around until its prow, Dix realized, seemed to be bobbing directly towards her. Dix picked up her binoculars for a closer look.

The rower was a man, and the short, shaggy shape beside him was a dog, a golden retriever. The man wore a straw hat and a baggy, plaid bathing suit and he rowed in easy, languid strokes, as if he belonged to the tableau of curving beach and ocean. He rowed like an athlete, Dix thought. His dog sat beside him, looking towards shore. As she watched, the man turned and saw Dix looking at them. He waved and Dix put down her binoculars.

Dix felt slightly breathless. He looked like Roger, her ex-husband.

Maybe Roger had left his girlfriend on the ski hills of

Colorado and come back to claim her. Dix winced. There. Enough said. It wasn't as if Roger had dumped her. Dix was the one who'd left because Roger was jealous of Dix's writing. When Dix went to her room to work on her books, Roger moved furniture in the room below. Or he consoled himself by disappearing into his group of wealthy friends, his racquet club, his coke habit. Dix had felt like a spy with Roger. A double agent, collecting information about the rich for the ordinary person. She was startled to realize that somebody like Roger brooded about having credibility because his inheritance made what he did look token.

Dix sighed and stared through the binoculars again. The glasses were handsomely made and easily picked up the stranger and even the name of his yacht anchored further out. Under its flag, Dix read the words: *Gone Away, Wilmington, North Carolina.*

Perhaps the man had seen her from his boat and decided to come ashore and meet her. He looked close to her age. A plausible companion in a straw hat and plaid bathing suit. A dog owner even. Maybe he was a gift from the ocean, Dix thought. A Christmas offering who would put a stop to that whispery little voice from snickering: *a woman without a man is a nobody.*

At the airport, the same whispery voice had told Dix to buy the how-to book with a title in embossed jade letters: *How to Find Your Soul Mate*. "Your own special someone desires to be with you as much as you wish to be with him or her," the jacket said. On the flight, Dix had escaped to the toilet with the book, leaving Emma playing with her Barbies. As she read, Dix began to sob into a paper towel. She didn't hear the angry knocks on the door because the book's hopeful words had made her weep. "You don't meet your soul mate until you are ready"—the book assured Dix—"until you are the partner you'd like to find."

Dix smiled to herself. At the rate I'm going, I'll be in my nineties, she thought.

Now the stranger's raft was at the sandbar where Emma was swimming. Emma, her darling girl, whose joy in the ocean made Dix feel humble. But where was Emma? Ah, there—between the man in the dinghy and the shore—rising out of a swollen green wave, holding something aloft in both arms. Dix could hear Emma whooping as she leaped and bobbed, carrying a small honey-coloured object high above her curly head.

Dix was suddenly conscious of Sarasvati watching her from the edge of the yoga platform. Dix couldn't see the yoga class. They must be on their backs, relaxing in corpse position. Dix shuddered. Sarasvati was scowling as if Dix was somebody she didn't like—a tourist woman who walked the beach, looking for men in yachts.

Well, what if I do talk to the man? Dix thought. There was no rule at the ashram against socializing, was there? Besides, Dix already felt as if she knew the stranger who was pulling up his dinghy down the shore, his shaggy, golden dog bouncing around him. He even moved like Roger who felt at ease around boats and dogs.

Dix wondered if he came from a wealthy family too. And if he grew supercilious and cold, like Roger, when you disagreed with him.

Dix waved at the stranger who stood down the shore putting a leash on his retriever. He was taller than she'd guessed with lean, muscled calves like a soccer player. Would he be disappointed now that he could see her? Or would he admire the way her yellow bikini arched across her high, smooth hips?

The stranger waved back, but he didn't come over. Instead, he sat down in the sand and pulled something out of a knapsack and began to eat. Dix waved again, disappointed.

"Mommy, look! It's got teeth!" Emma said and Dix

forced herself to examine Emma's conch again. The shell around its spongy little foot wasn't a deep labial pink like the other ones Emma found but a shocking bloody orange and its lips were ribbed with black and white ridges.

"It won't hurt you, Emmy," Dix smiled.

"Mrs. O'Connell—I want a word with you!" someone called.

Dix turned. Sarasvati seemed to be floating towards them, her ankle-length orange robes dragging in the sand.

"Emma has found something rare," Dix called. "Do you know what it is?"

"These creatures can't live out of the ocean," Sarasvati called back. You must tell her to put it back."

She didn't smile at Dix and Dix felt a small shock. "Mommy, don't talk to that lady." Emma bumped her forehead against Dix's stomach. "She's mean."

"Sssh, Emmy. Be nice." Dix put her hand on her stomach so Emma couldn't bump it.

Sarasvati's face puffed up. "Mrs. O'Connell? You signed our pledge, didn't you?"

"Yes, I signed the pledge," Dix sighed.

"Have you forgotten it is against our beliefs to take life?" Sarasvati snapped.

Dix shook her head. She wanted to defend Emma, but over the noise of the frothing turquoise waves, Sarasvati sounded forceful and terrifying, and Dix felt suddenly listless, as if she was turning to sand. She felt embarassed because people on the beach were looking at them.

The man from North Carolina had stopped eating his lunch. His flat, open face was looking her way with concern. Behind him, two boys in orange life jackets and a water-ski instructor were watching them too.

"Please, Mommy! Let me keep her!" Emma cried. "Her name is Esmeralda and she doesn't have anyone to play with."

"If you hang on to things, Emma, you only get hurt," Sarasvati said angrily.

"Mommy! I want to keep Esmeralda!" Emma whimpered.

"Oh, I'm just sick and tired of you people!" Sarasvati spun around and strode off back to her class.

Dix noticed the stranger waving at her and pointing to something, but Dix ignored him and stared at Sarasvati, longing for the older woman to turn around and say Emma could keep her shell. Instead, the swami kept her back to Dix. There was a bustle of arms and legs as

Sarasvati ordered her students to lie in *matsyasana*, the fish position—elbows behind their backs, chests arched. Sarasvati's voice sounded very cross now. Few of the campers were supple enough to do the *asanas* properly, let alone appreciate the teachings of Swami Sevada whose round, pop-out eyes on the sign above the platform seemed to beg everyone to be patient.

Then Dix saw the small figure running down the beach.

"Emma! Stop!" Dix yelled, but she knew Emma couldn't hear her over the noise of the surf.

Up ahead, Emma was attracting looks from nude sunbathers eating their Christmas buffet under the Club Med umbrellas. As Emma ran by, clutching her shell, a topless woman lifted her glass.

"Go, kid, go!" she called. The woman's breasts were large and sunburnt and she stood with a man in a leopard skin bikini. When Dix jogged past, the pair stared disapprovingly. Dix kept her eyes glumly ahead on Emma.

Emma must—there was really no other choice, Dix thought—Emma *must* give up her conch shell. The little creature in the shell had a right to live like everything else. Besides, if she and Emma were thrown out of the ashram, Dix would have problems finding them a room over Christmas.

Underfoot, the sand felt soft and loose and Dix slowed her pace. If only we could leave, Dix thought. It had been a mistake to come. The ashram's regime was too rigid for a child and Emma hated its vegetarian Hindu food, so every afternoon Dix took her down the beach for a hamburger.

Dix had first seen Paradise Island the Christmas she was thirteen — before the developers had built their casinos. Dix had spied its empty, windswept tip from her Nassau hotel room and vowed to visit it when she was grown up. That same Christmas, Dix developed a crush on the elevator boy. Her parents had told Dix to forget him. "When you come down to the islands with your husband," her mother had laughed, "the elevator boy will be your doorman."

She must have come down just to prove her mother wrong. It was the sort of ornery thing divorced people did. The elevator boy was probably an official in the Ministry of Tourism by now.

The wind was blowing the foil off the synthetic pine outside the Holiday Inn when Dix caught up to Emma.

"Emma! You bad girl!" Dix grabbed the straps at the back of Emma's Speedo. "You're going to be sorry."

The heads of a few volleyball players spun round.

"Don't hurt me, Mommy!" Emma shrieked. She hurled herself out of Dix's hands and ran squealing into the ocean. One of the volleyball players yelled something at them, but Dix didn't stop to listen.

She threw herself at Emma and grabbed her around the waist and Emma fell face first into the water, pulling Dix down on top of her. Emma sank down quickly. God damn her, Dix thought. And god damn Christmas. Emma wasn't even trying to swim because she didn't want to drop the conch.

Kicking hard, Dix rolled off Emma.

"Mommy!" Emma's head broke the surface. She was choking on seawater. "I want my Daddy!"

Dix felt herself sag.

"Oh, Emmy. I'm sorry."

Dix kissed the top of Emma's head and hugged her, and then she noticed the stranger. She groaned. He was standing on the shore with the volleyball players who'd stopped their game to watch. The stranger waved his straw hat. Dix didn't wave back. Slowly, her head down, Dix walked back to shore, holding Emma's hand.

The yellow retriever bounded towards them as they came out of the ocean.

"Y'all! Watch out! Bellaire's got loose!" the stranger called.

The dog leapt up on Emma, bumping the shell out of Emma's hand with its nose.

"Mommy! Make it get down!" Emma squealed.

Dix grabbed the dog's trailing leash and the man rushed over and squatted down beside Emma.

"Honey, if Bellaire jumps up again, just say Sit in the meanest old voice you can and give her fanny a big push down." He pressed his dog's haunches firmly down.

"Are you sure?" Emma said.

"Uh-huh. Bellaire loves kids." He winked at Dix as he stood up, and Dix noticed that his plaid bathing suit had slipped down on his hips so she could see the long finger-shaped dimples on either side of his torso, just above his hipbones. Dix loved these dimples on men's bellies—it made their skin look soft and babyish, like bread that some woman had touched, knowing her fingers would leave tell-tale indentations.

"Hello. I'm Dix, Emma's mother." Dix waited for some sign of coldness, or disapproval about the way she'd acted.

But he only took off his straw hat and walked over grinning. Dix felt herself get breathless again. He did look a little like her ex-husband, Roger. The same broad face and blond hair. Except the tan made his eyes appear strangely bright, as if he was lit up from inside.

"I'm Brian L. Farrell. The *L* is for General Lee, of course."

He laughed at his own joke on himself. At least, he didn't talk like Roger, Dix thought. His southern drawl made him sound, well—harmless, like a child who hadn't learned grown-up talk.

He was holding Emma's conch.

"Your daughter's one lucky girl!"

"Oh, what is it?" shrieked Emma.

"A Flame Helmet," Brian said and gave it back to Emma. "The fishermen sell them to the States so people can use them for cameo brooches."

"Oh, Mommy," Emma said. "Do I really have to throw it back?"

"Emmy, it'll be happier in the sea," Dix said. She realized she was still staring at Brian. Actually, he didn't resemble Roger at all, Dix thought. The look in his strange, bright eyes was guarded, as if he expected people to disappoint him. She felt suddenly tender towards him.

"No, Mommy! I want to keep Esmeralda!" Emma cried.

"Hooray for Emma!" he said. "She's a big girl! She'll do what's right! You agree, don't you, Bellaire?" The dog jumped up and licked his hand.

Emma giggled. Brian handed her a stick.

"Throw it for Bellaire!"

Emma tossed it into the whitecaps and the three of them watched the retriever snatch up the stick and shake off its coat before dropping it at Emma's feet. Brian laughed.

"Bellaire sure likes you!"

Emma laughed too. "Mr.—would you—"

"Brian."

"Brian, would you drop Esmeralda in the ocean— way out?" Emma held up her shell. "Where nobody can find her?"

He smiled. "Well, this calls for a special Christmas celebration. Let's put Esmeralda in a pail and drop her out past the lighthouse!"

"Oh, Mommy! Can we?" Emma said.

"Emmy, I told Sarasvati I'd help make some chupatis for the Christmas feast," Dix said softly.

"Yuck!" Emma said.

"Well, why don't y'all finish your chores and *then* we'll go have turkey sandwiches on my boat." Brian tapped her arm as if they were old buddies. "All right, Dix?"

His fingers felt dry and warm, and Dix could feel herself weakening. She wanted to please him. She wanted to go with him.

"Hell, you can do your holy granola on the deck. I won't mind." He tightened his grip on her arm.

"What?" Dix said.

"The kooky stuff y'all practise here." Brian repeated the words on the ashram sign: "Proper exercise, proper breathing, proper relaxation, proper diet—" He chuckled. "Maybe I'll become a yogi too."

Dix looked down at her feet. "I don't think so."

"No, Mommy!" Emma groaned. "I want to go now!"

"What about tomorrow then? Come to my marina at Hurricane Hole."

"Oh, please, please, Mommy!" Emma cried.

Dix shook her head.

"Dix, if you change your mind—"He shrugged and put on his straw hat.

All at once Dix felt sad, as if he'd refused her something. Quickly, she put on her sunglasses so Brian and

Emma wouldn't see the tears filling her eyes and scanned the beach for Sarasvati. The swami was nowhere to be seen, but a few campers still lingered on the yoga platform. They were waving at the old refugee ship she'd noticed that morning. It was sailing by, ploughing through the waves, just beyond the string of orange buoys by the swimmers' area.

On the deck, hundreds of people were jumping up and down around a man beating a drum. Some of them were drinking from bottles and yelling "Merry Christmas" to the people on the shore. Dix waved at them. She wondered how the refugees could be so happy if they didn't know where they were going.

She was going to ask Brian what he thought of their chances, but he was no longer beside her. He was putting Esmeralda in the dinghy.

I could still change my mind, Dix thought. I could call him back and tell him we'll go with him, but he'd turned his back to her and was whooping and hollering at Emma who was helping him push his raft into the ocean.

Listlessly, Dix watched Brian climb into his dinghy.

"Goodbye!" she called. He couldn't hear. He was already rowing away.

At sunset, the day after Boxing Day, Dix thought she saw the yacht from North Carolina go through the busy channel by the lighthouse. She'd wanted to go to his marina, but she couldn't seem to move from the camp, and Emma didn't mind because she'd made friends with a boy from New York. He and Emma were playing near the yoga platform where Sarasvati was teaching a class. The swami hadn't seemed especially interested or surprised when Dix had told her about Emma giving up the shell.

Most swamis felt they could lash out at the campers if they felt frustrated, a guest had told Dix at the Christmas feast. Sevada himself used to do it. If you were a devotee, you wrote off these incidents as a trial to test your patience. Dix didn't agree and she avoided Sarasvati after that, although Dix still felt envious when meditation was over and the swami asked someone else to pass around the bowl of fruit and nuts.

Dix picked up her binoculars. The setting sun was blazing right into her eyes, but she managed to pick out the name *Gone Away* on the yacht's stern. The yacht was gliding along in tandem with two other boats—an ocean liner whose gargantuan smokestack was shaped like a fish tail, and a slate-coloured freighter named *Eastore*.

Dix had heard a radio announcer talking about the freighter on her Sony Walkman that morning: it was deporting hundreds of illegal refugees back to Haiti.

She trained her glasses now on the deck of *Gone Away* and waited, and sure enough, in a few moments, Brian appeared in his baggy plaid bathing suit. He was talking to a crew member who handed him something that looked like a pail. He leaned out and tilted it over the water. He could have been tipping garbage overboard, for all she knew, but Dix hoped he was dropping Emma's Flame Helmet into the deepest part of the ocean, just as he said he would.

Dix sighed. She put down the binoculars. One day, if Emma asked about their first Christmas alone, she would say: That was the year we sent our treasures back to the sea. Don't you remember? We had everything we needed.

It really wasn't so terrible to be on your own, she thought. Emma and I manage. And manage was a better word than happy. It implied effort and success without laying claim to anything more.

All at once Dix felt light-hearted and something else. What was it? Gratitude to Brian for taking the shell? Ah—of all things, Dix felt relief, an inkling that she had been spared. Humming, Dix picked up the binoculars again. She watched Brian's yacht bounce easily past the freighter crowded with refugees and then disappear behind the fish-tailed ocean liner.

That night Dix dreamt she was still on the beach, looking through her binoculars. And far out beyond the shore where Dix sat, yes, way past the single parasailor drifting high above the curve of blond sand, beyond the lighthouse and the turquoise channel with the yacht from North Carolina and the gargantuan liner and the freighter bearing the refugees nobody wanted, oh miles out towards the western horizon where the sun was setting over the darkening ocean, Dix saw a giant golden conch burst out of the waves in a cascade of seawater and surge majesterially up to the heavens. It was only a dream, but all the same, right before her eyes, Dix was astonished to see the shell change into a large honey-coloured breast. And for a moment, only a second and no more, the breast plashed droplets of a gorgeous golden orange. Then it vanished into the dying light.

Young and Gay

I MARRIED Billie down there. At a little Presbyterian church Billie liked. Billie! Not Jacob! Of course, I hadn't seen or heard from Billie for fifty-four years when he asked me to marry him. First, Billie sent me a letter saying his wife had died and Billie had heard Jacob was gone and would I like to get together and talk about old times. I didn't think I would. Would you want an old boyfriend to see you after fifty-four years? Would you want to see him? All those wrinkles! Go on. You would not. But I said yes. I married Billie when I was seventy-six and I hadn't seen him for fifty-four years!

I flew down to Fort Lauderdale on a Saturday, and then Billie and I went out with Billie's cousin, Hi, that night, and Hi got awfully tight too and fell down in the dining room of the Holiday Inn, and Billie had to carry him out of the hotel! Oh, I had a lovely introduction to the South.

On Monday, Billie and I were married, and I made all the food for our reception. I did everything! Billie didn't have any idea how you do things, so I arranged for flowers and telegrams and made tuna sandwiches, which are the only kind I know how to make.

And Hi got quite tight again and drove Billie's Ford so it screeched around the corners, and then Billie got a bit tight and toasted me with a glass of champagne. "Here's to our first child, Madeleine," Billie said. Billie was eighty-one.

For supper that night Billie cooked me a chop. We didn't have champagne again but I didn't care. As long as I had Billie, I didn't care what I ate or where I was.

I can't say what I specifically liked about him. About Billie. I just liked him. When we first met way back when, I was singing at a party and Billie was playing the piano. Billie asked Uncle Mac if he could take me to the movies. I rode on the handlebars of Billie's bike.

Uncle Mac used to say, "Madeleine, you marry that fellow and you're going to have your garden filled up with white-haired pickaninnies!" As if I cared that Billie was dark skinned! Because he was. Oh, very. Billie was very dark skinned. And I had white hair. I have had white hair and no eyebrows since I was twenty. I hate it. It makes me look like a cat. I have to draw eyebrows in with a black pencil. Billie used to call me the White Indian because of my hair and the way I liked my gin-and-anything. Wait! That's a lie. Billie never called me that. Jacob did.

Billie's apartment in Fort Lauderdale was tiny. He and I didn't live in the top places, you know. We had just four rooms. A living room/dining room (apartments always have that in Lauderdale), and a wee kitchen off it, and a bedroom and a bathroom. And an air conditioner I hated and wouldn't let Billie use.

We were on a field. Right on a huge field with the highway behind. So you know how noisy it was. As Charlie Mathews said when he took his first look at Billie's apartment, "Well, Madeleine, it's adequate." Charlie knew the kind of big house I was used to living in, with all my nice things. Up north, my position is assured. But I didn't have any position down there. None whatsoever.

At the back door, I had a garden. How big was it? Nine by four. A nine-by-four garden, and I used to manage two backyards of roses! Well, sir, I planted everything in my Lauderdale garden, but only crazy things grew there. Like the wildflowers from the field. And I had some lovely begonias.

Of course, I didn't know anybody. You don't get to know people in Lauderdale. You can play bridge with them, but you don't know anything about their backgrounds. It's a different standard. Nobody except Billie and I and the Beechams were married. Well, maybe I am an odd person, but I didn't give a hoot about the goings-on.

Because I was never bored in Lauderdale. Not ever. In the morning, I cooked breakfast. Quite a big one: we had a little meat, hamburgers maybe, and I'd fry up potatoes if there were cold ones in the fridge. And I got Billie to like tea! We ate on trays in twin beds and watched that man from Canada on the television. Dirk something. He gave us the Canadian news every morning.

After breakfast, Billie and I got dressed at our leisure and went out shopping in Billie's Buick. Sometimes Billie took his car in for a wash. Or I had him drive me to Pier One to look at white china. Lauderdale is where I bought the cats I have on the rad in my TV room. The white cats. What other colour would they be? My son

Rick used to say, "If you sit still, Mother will paint you white." I would, you know. I painted everything white way back when I was Jacob's wife. And Billie said all the white doodads in our Lauderdale apartment gave him snowblindness.

Then Billie and I came home from shopping and had lunch while we watched a soap on the telly. Maybe we'd hold hands. The Beechams used to tease me about what happened when Billie took off his hearing aid and I took off my glasses. I couldn't see Billie and he couldn't hear me, and you know . . .

What did one old man say to the other old man when they passed a pretty girl on the street? (Everybody's heard this chestnut, but what do I care?) Why, the old man said, "Doesn't that girl remind you of something we used to do?" And the other old fella said, "She sure does, but for the life of me I can't remember what!"

Then Billie and I had a lie-down, and afterwards we got dressed and went out or sat in the garden and had a cup of tea. Then I might have a swim.

The Beechams called me the Polar Bear—not because of my hair, but because I went in swimming all winter. Nobody in Lauderdale swims in what they call the cool months, even though the temperature is seventy-eight degrees.

The Beechams were the only people I knew well. They ran a 7-Eleven store in Lauderdale. That's like a Mac's Milk. Imagine me knowing a man who runs a Mac's Milk! And Sally Beecham used to mind it, and I would go to her apartment and cook dinner while she looked after the store. I liked the Beechams. They took me to the racetrack. Billie never went—it was too much standing for him. But I had a good time.

Then the Beechams bought a house with an orange tree in the yard. Billie and I moved too, because Billie didn't like the people in our building. We had a mafia man living next door. There'd be people visiting him at all hours—that's how Billie knew what he was. The mafia man didn't have a wife. He was a big, blond man and he always had a new mistress in for the weekend. I don't know what the mistresses looked like—I never saw them, they never went out. The maid who came to clean said the mafia man had a Japanese house over on Palm Court, right on the water. It was a very expensive Japanese house with twenty phones in it, and something must have gone wrong for him to move to our building. The maid's name was Size and she was a size all right!

There was the man dressed as a clergyman who lived with a woman who wasn't his wife, and he was no clergyman. And that other couple—nice young people who got out in the night without paying their rent. I liked them too. And the man who lived to the left of them—he lived with a woman, and one morning I got up early to swim and saw the fellow throwing the woman out of their apartment, and she had nothing on but a nightie!

Come to think of it, it was an awful bunch in that apartment building. I left out the man who ran around naked along the balconies at night! He'd see an attractive woman and run back and forth on her balcony. Billie looked too formidable for him to think about doing that to me!

There were rats too. Mrs. Size found a nest of them under Billie's bed. The caretakers of the apartment building had left our door open, and the rats got in. They were like that, the woman and her husband who ran the place. She was dying, the poor thing. I used to take her flowers. She had no children.

Billie and I moved to a motel, a nice motel right on the ocean, and the last year in Lauderdale I was in the ocean every day. Oh, I had a good time. I was crazy about Billie and we had a good time together. You know, I can't remember thinking Billie was going to die. I just didn't think about it. It never crossed my mind. I just thought, it's lovely to go south with Billie.

When Billie first wrote and asked if he could come and see me, I wrote Billie back and said, "There's no fool like an old fool, so you might as well come up." Billie wouldn't get a shock at my white hair, now would he? So Billie flew up to Toronto and drove a rented car all the way from the airport just to see me in my little town near Petrolia. He came into the TV room in my big house, wearing a straw boater and carrying a cane. And I had Janet come over. Billie knew Janet when we used to ride on the handlebars of Billie's bike.

Oh, we had the usual gin-and-anything, and then we had a fine dinner. Billie played my piano and did tricks with his cane, and he said to Janet, "You know, I'm going to take our White Indian back to Fort Lauderdale with me." Janet's so stupid, she didn't know what to say. And I thought Billie was joking. He'd always been a bit of a joker.

And when you think of it, I might have walked into anything. Marrying Billie! Not Jacob! I married Jacob when I was twenty-five. I married Billie when I was seventy-six and hadn't seen him for fifty-four years! And for ten winters, Billie and I went down to Lauderdale about the 16th of October and came up around the 7th of May. Billie died five years ago, and I haven't been south since. But I liked it in Lauderdale. Oh, I had a fine time! I was young and gay.

cyber

Cyber Tales

One Night,
Very Late,
And Saddened
by a Recent
Heartbreak,
I Was Cruising
Cyber Space

O NE NIGHT, very late, and saddened by a recent heartbreak, I was cruising Cyber Space when a sandalled foot appeared on my screen. And then the hem of a long golden robe and lo—Aphrodite rose up out of the monitor. She told me my years of seeking romantic thrills had left me depressed and in need of comfort. There were millions like me, she said, helplessly following their desire from one partner to the next without getting the satisfaction they longed to find. She pointed laughingly to a small mound at the top of my palm which she claimed was my girdle of Venus. "It's the fault of our goddess-driven natures," she said. "But I'm middle-aged," I told her. "Shouldn't I be past this sort of thing?" "We are never without the need for romance," she smiled. "Or stories which are the best cure for those like us who lose our way in love." She told me not to be frightened but she had come to take me to meet the others like myself who fall in love too easily. She said they were from many places and time periods and liked nothing better than to sit at their keyboards, e-mailing each other their stories. "They're waiting for you now," she said. "In a little chat room I know." Reluctantly, I let her take my trembling hand . . .

Click on E to enter *Row Man.CITY*

The *Row Man.CITY* Chat Room

Helen of Troy: So, girls, let's start dissing—

Goth girl: The Neanderthal guys.

Aphrodite: I only go out with gods myself.

The Tyrant of Assyria: You poor chick!

Gertrude Stein: Who let *him* into Romance City?

Ariadne: I think the tyrant's going to tell the first tale.

Aphrodite: No, I am. And here it is—for all of us who like the pleasures of intermission . . .

```
*Row Man.CITY*
Msg #49998
From: Aphrodite
To: All
Subj: VIRGINS
```

virgins

Have you ever met a virgin
you couldn't love?
    - Aphrodite

How I Tried to Save a Saint

Athens

MY OLD FRIEND Saint Paul was finishing off a large Greek salad when he said: "Aphrodite . . . I am a . . . a virgin."

"You poor, lonely mortal!" I exclaimed and ordered him another plate of red mullet.

I am who Saint Paul said I am—Aphrodite, and he was, first of all, a tent maker, with fine olive skin and garlic breath that none of us dared mention.

"How did this come to happen?"

Saint Paul shook his head. It was a long story, he said, but he just hadn't got around to it. For all sorts of reasons. His parents' death on a sea voyage to Sicily. His one and only fiancée was stoned to death for her religious beliefs in Ephesus, Asia Minor. He'd always planned to marry and have a family, but he'd just let things slide after he lost his fiancée. Besides, he worked so hard organizing his band of Christians, there wasn't time for love.

"In fact, I was hoping . . . " Saint Paul started in on the mullet. "I was hoping that you and I . . . well, you know, Aphrodite . . . that you would be the one to end my sorry state."

"Oh!" I said. "I see." I only said "I see" to hide the fact that it had never—no, not once—occurred to me to think of Saint Paul in a sexual way. He was a Christian, after all, and there was his breath to consider, although his olive skin looked silky to the touch and might, with a little effort, be considered pleasing.

"Not that I would ever marry a pagan like yourself." He was smiling in a kindly way I found annoying.

"Well?" he asked. "Would you?"

I slid my hand out from under his. Saint Paul had sweaty hands. That was another thing I'd noticed.

"You know me," I sighed. "I am the goddess who

helps men. Any time you want. Just give me the word."

"What a lucky break!" said Saint Paul. "I'll look you up at your next love festival in Corinth."

Corinth

My love festival started off slowly. The line-up of men ran all the way down from Acro-Corinth to the town. I am frightened of heights, so my temple is set in the bowl of the mountaintop, between two rock outcroppings.

In the stoa, my girls were offering the tired pilgrims all the things I love best in the world to eat. Golden apples, passion-red pomegranates, wedges of wild honey and feta cheese. A broiled lamb, several smoked pigs.

Saint Paul avoided the four-mile queue and came straight over to me.

I was standing in my temple doorway, where the shadows trap the cool air. I never stand on the ramparts. Why make myself dizzy looking down at the Gulf of Corinth shining like a blue death so far below?

"What a surprise to see you at our religious festivities!" I said. I noticed the front of his toga was soaking. Obviously, Saint Paul was not used to mountain hikes.

"It's now or never!" my old friend replied breathlessly.

"Later," I said and waved at a gyro of mutton. "Are you hungry?"

"I don't eat pagan meat."

"This is from the Saronic Gulf," I said. "Very fresh."

"Yes, I know," said Saint Paul. "But women put it on your altar before this ceremony. I refuse to eat lamb that has been offered to pagan idols." He removed his sweaty toga. "You should honour something higher than yourself."

"Old friend, you know I don't separate matter and spirit," I said. "There is nothing higher than our physical selves."

"Wrong, wrong, wrong," Saint Paul put on the fresh robe my girl brought him. "But never mind. You are only a woman."

I helped Saint Paul to some retsina, thinking, Ignore his insults. The poor man's climbed all the way up here, so now he's hot and cross. Be patient. He's counting on your help.

After all, you are the descendant of Gaia, the great goddess, who stands for love — the all-enduring power of the universe.

You have a reputation to uphold, Aphrodite. Wasn't it you who handed Hippomenes three golden apples to win Atalanta? And didn't you breathe life into Pygmalion's ivory statue?

You owe Saint Paul *this*.

For being an orphan.

For losing his fiancée.

For being a man!

Because he wants you!

I grabbed up a handful of black olives, thinking, Yes, Aphrodite—You are Saint Paul's last hope.

"I hope you didn't mind what I said about pagan meat." Saint Paul slung his arm around me. Roughly. He nuzzled my neck.

I almost fell into the propylaea.

How could I tell my old friend that he reeked of the shrimps my girls had brought him? It was all I could do to keep myself from shaking.

"Why don't you read some Sappho," I said and lowered myself to my couch. "It will put us in the mood."

"You're not changing your mind, are you, Aphrodite?"

"No, of course not," I said crossly. "You know me better than that."

"Yes," he said, smiling. "I do."

"'I shall burn the fat thigh bones of a white she-goat on her altar . . .'"

"No, no!" I snapped. "Leave out the pagan meat."

Saint Paul began again: "'I confess I love that which caresses me . . .'"

"Better," I murmured.

"You look beautiful, Aphrodite. Except for your peplos. Can you take it off?"

I made no reply. By then, I was feigning sleep.

With one eye open, I saw Leto, my Roman slave, come into the room.

"I must ask you to leave," I heard her tell Saint Paul. "The festivities have worn Aphrodite out."

My old friend looked if not disappointed, somehow resigned, well—he looked like Saint Paul again. He told Leto he'd come back in the morning.

Only the next day I was too ill to get off my couch. Leto said I had to stay put. She said I couldn't see Saint Paul either.

"You've got to stop this nursemaid stuff," she said. "I thought you are devoted to pleasure."

"I . . . I am."

"Then tell him no."

"I can't," I said. "I promised him I would."

"Aphrodite, a mercy fuck is a sin against the gods," Leto said. "Surely you know that?"

"That's not how Paul would see it," I said. "And there is only one god as far as he is concerned."

"The very thought of sex with this Christian is making you sick."

"Leto, if I go through with this, the future of the world may be different."

"He'll only see you as a whore. Now you tell him you're not going to go through with it while I sit here and listen."

"I—no—all right. I'm thinking."

Leto poured me a glass of Metaxa and called in Saint Paul.

"Aphrodite!" Saint Paul said. "At last!"

"Dear friend," I said. "I . . . I have something to say that I can't—"

"I didn't sleep at all last night," Saint Paul said. "The music, the snakes—and outside my door, one of your girls kept striking people with a branch of myrtle."

He smiled. "Thank Jehovah, you are here to make me feel better."

He began to jump up and down like a child.

"Saint Paul, our religious differences—" I waved at

the remains of the feast which Leto had left on my banquet table. Some melons from Aegina, a half-eaten rump of mutton. "They turn out to be more important than I thought. You understand, don't you?"

"You mean you are going back on your word!" Saint Paul said.

I looked at Leto and Leto nodded.

"I—I—that's one way of putting it. Yes."

Saint Paul placed one of his sweaty hands on my cheek.

"Aphrodite, it's such a long way home."

Leto scowled. "Please tell my mistress you have no hard feelings."

"Of course not." Saint Paul looked indignant. "A Christian knows how to forgive. Right, Aphrodite?"

"Yes, no hard feelings," I said and followed him to the processional path where Leto had tethered his donkey.

I stood on the ramparts and watched Saint Paul ride off. The Saronic Gulf lay miles below like a pool of blue ice but I felt no dizziness. The faraway cliffs shimmered gold with swallowed light.

Then I heard the sound of flutes and trumpets. Leto and the others placed the roasted she-goat on my altar.

They sang an invocation to Priapus, dancing hand in hand around me. Down the hill, the line of men shuffled forward.

```
(R)eply, (E)mail reply, follow
(T)hread, (P)revious or (N)ext n
```

one—

night

I, Naram-Sin, the Tyrant of
Assyria, Lord of Four
Quarters of the Earth,
strongman and hero, am the
second person to log onto
Row Man.CITY with stories
that will edify and teach all
who come here.

stands

I Am the
Tyrant of
Assyria and
I Kneel
Prostrate at
Your Restless,
Modern Feet

DO I BORE YOU, GIRL?" I said as I lay naked on her paisley sheets. I had on my funny ziggurat hat. The one with a reception ramp for my descending gods.

I am only a king, Naram-Sin, Lord of Four Quarters of the Earth, strongman and hero. I do not know what great literature is. I come from the Land of Two Rivers, the Tigris and the Euphrates. Five thousand men dine every night at my palace. I am not what you are used to. You like my body, but are you sure you want the great ruler who is attached to it? You are a flexible woman. I knew that soon after I met you.

You slept with me so fast, girl! One hour after meeting!

As I have said many times to my people, I need somebody who is flexible to go back with me to the Land of Ur. So I can do the king thing and feel at ease. I want you to meet my daughters. They can learn a lot from you, girl. And they will help you with your style of dress. Your clothing needs work. And your strange hair. You know it does. A few hours with my court dresser—that's all it will take. And me at your side—Naram-Sin, Lord of Four Quarters of the Earth, strongman and hero—day in and day out. I am a lover of lapis lazuli, I eat the meat of young bears, I like to watch lions fight in the streets of my capital. These are things you should know so you can decide if you want the great ruler who kneels prostrate at your restless, modern feet.

My palace is like the one you see in your history books. Only noisier, with smells you moderns should learn to remember. When I am not at war, we will have sex five times a day. Already my people are dying to meet you. Oh, girl, I am just bowled over by the way you sunbathe without your top or get hot when I say, "Let's plough the field, praise Ishtar, let's fertilize the earth!"

Do you make fun of my Assyrian accent behind my back? I don't care. I will work on getting rid of it. Do I bore you, girl? I will improve myself for you. I will let nothing get in my way until you are satisfied with the Lord who rules the Great Lands of the River Valley. I am talking empires here.

Babylon, Elam, Eden. I will destroy them all. Because I love you. Oh, girl, I don't care if you are only having sex with me because I am the Tyrant of Assyria. The fifth to be exact, in a long line. I have monuments to my glory set up everywhere. And yet you sleep around, girl, you sleep around. I am not an unfaithful man. I am not like you. I can only plough the earth with somebody I love.

I know it is not what you expected to a hear a man like me say. Considering my titles . . . King of Akkad and

Kish, priest of Anu, viceroy of Inanna, the chosen of Enlil . . . Do I bore you? I can't wait to show you our ancient ways—I can't wait to show you how to throw a spear so it doesn't pull your arm from its socket. And other things you can only guess at, girl.

(R)eply, (E)mail reply, follow
(T)hread, (P)revious or (N)ext n

hot

guys

```
*Row Man.CITY*
Msg #94291
From: Ariadne
To: The Tyrant of Assyria
Subj: HOT GUYS
```

I'm honoured to be the third
story-teller to pass on a
cyber tale. This is for you,
Ariadne Naram-Sin.

Ariadne
Was a Party
Animal

THE THIGHS of Theseus are what I saw first when he passed me on his motorbike. I was riding in a Cretan taxi. I looked out the taxi window and I saw those thighs and I thought, I want that.

Theseus looked just like the statues in the national museum at Athens. Do you know the ones I mean? The shapely, long-limbed marble boys who tower above your head?

At Knossos, the door to the palace was locked. God damn. God damn fuck. Theseus kicked the door. Once. Twice. It opened.

I was lying in my pyjamas listening to a Sony Walkman.

"I've come to save you, Ariadne," he said.

"Way to go, Thes!" I handed him a packet of matches. The string I gave him to find his way out of the labyrinth was the second thing I handed him.

Only he didn't kill the Minotaur. There was no need—the poor thing was so lonely, he'd follow us anywhere.

The next time I handed Theseus some matches, he was the one lying down. In our hotel room in Naxos—the Hotel Minos, for God's sake. Theseus was pleased I'd found a cheap room near the portera. It's a Naxian landmark—the old marble doorway leading nowhere.

"A light, Ariadne?" he said.

"Again?" I threw him my lighter and lay down on the bed. Our window opened onto the harbour and its long, white sail-sized curtains snapped and cracked so wildly, I could have sworn we were on the sea.

The next day Theseus left for Athens while I was sleeping.

Big deal.

The very same afternoon the Minotaur and I took the ferry to Santorini where there's more wine than water. I said I was looking for Theseus but I was only killing time. There's not a lot to do in the islands.

In Santorini, the Minotaur sat behind me on the motor scooter and wouldn't stop laughing at the snake-like shadows his long hair and tail made on the roadside cliff.

I don't think Theseus had let the Minotaur ride his bike before.

We ate a Greek salad in Oia and then zoomed up to the monastery of Pirgos. The Minotaur got vertigo and wanted to leave.

"Hang tight," I said and the Minotaur whinnied all the way down the slope to Red Beach.

We lay in the sun. The Minotaur wore nothing. I wore a gold bikini. The Minotaur was very hot, and when he stood up all I could see were the pillars of his bull-like thighs sliding away from me up to the clouds.

And I could have sworn my head was a bottle opener. My head can be bent back by the weight of giant phalluses.

Later, I held the Minotaur in my arms on the boat to Mykonos where we were going for a little party action.

"I can't wait to loaf all day with you on the wind-surfers' beach," I told him. "And toast your hairy beauty at the Caprice Bar where the sunset is the best in the world."

And still later, on Paros, in the Valley of the Butter-flies, I told him he was the one I'd been looking for all along.

In the cooling twilight breeze, as the lovesick butter-flies fluttered up into the evening sky, I said I'd never leave him. And he—the poor beast—he cried.

```
(R)eply, (E)mail reply, follow
(T)hread, (P)revious or (N)ext n
```

hot

Allow me to introduce myself
as Marilyn, the "Great Date"
of the century. Listed on
the next page for your
evaluation and comment is
a statement of my assets
and/or liabilities.

dates

I Am Not
a Bottle
Blonde

TENACIOUSLY SURVIVED a deprived childhood

Connoisseur of old inns and Chardonnays from California

Combines a dovelike reticence and manic vivacity

Refuses to make love for less than three hours

Favourite tune—the old Hebrew spiritual, "Go Down Moses"

World-renown movie star

Has mixed feelings on ambivalence

Knows about hair dye: "I am not a bottle blonde. If you're a real blonde, people don't see anything wrong with helping Nature along."

Has a weakness for father figures

Wears underpants a lot

Once considered changing her hair colour to Red
Penny, Ultraviolet, Mango, Cyclamen, Apricot Glow
and Amaranth

Still measures five feet five, 36-24-36, 118 lbs., and a
size 12

Trustworthy, loyal, helpful, friendly, courteous, kind,
cheerful, brave and clean

Survived first husband: "I cooked peas and carrots together every night because he liked the colours."

Doesn't think men would like her if she had brown hair

Left second husband who shared her first husband's
hatred of her career

Was abandoned by third: "He sat and held my toe and
we just looked into each other's eyes."

Resolutely humorous

Wonders why greed and avarice still dominate the world

Thinks her genitals occupy a place on her body directly
proportionate to Australia's position vis-à-vis the rest
of the world

Wishes she had more female friends: "Blondes are the
women in Technicolor who make other women feel
they are in black and white."

Looks even lovelier without make-up

Wants to write a significant history about the early days
of moving pictures

Believes in art, sex, Judaism and hairdressing

Lifetime quest: to bring more beauty to the world

Is not addicted to barbiturates any more

Exhibits screw-loose seriousness

Is often photographed with sun and sand to put men in
an adventurous holiday mood

Frequently talks too little, unless asked a probing question

Has a song in her heart

Will never tone her hair colour down

Is determined to keep her romantic convictions about
justice

Thinks every man will leave her sooner or later for a
young Vogue model

Is short on confidence, long on courage

Served honourably, heroically and unselfishly in Hollywood's finest combatant force: Twentieth Century
Fox

World-renown lips: "All women have my mouth now."

Other favourite sayings: "I want to be blonde all over"
and "Enjoy the day."

This e-mail was composed by Marilyn's favourite dating service, Darin's Date & Make Computer Inc., 150 Sullivan Street, New York City 10012. Marilyn fully guarantees all of the above. Knowing this, any decisions you make will be of your own volition and choice. You may reach her through Darin's office at 212-673-2030 evenings or days.

This next message is from the Tyrant of Assyria.

```
Why are you still looking for
men, girl? I am the Tyrant of
Assyria, Naram-Sin, Lord of Four
Quarters of the Earth, strongman
and hero, and I kneel prostrate
at your restless modern feet.
  - Naram
```

The very next message is Darin's dating service's response to the above.

```
DA> Your failure to read
DA> instructions astounds me.
DA> PLEASE approach Marilyn
```

DA> through the proper agency
    channel.

TY> I'd like to remind all of you
TY> that I come from a different
TY> time period. We do not yet
TY> have-

DA> Did your system go down?
DA> Tyrant, old boy, we wish you
DA> good luck and happy hunting
DA> in the never-ending quest for
DA> truth, happiness and the
DA> right woman.

(R)eply, (E)mail reply, follow
(T)hread, (P)revious or (N)ext n

Row Man.CITY
Msg #21986
From: Catherine the Great
To: Marilyn Monroe
Subj: SUPER STUDS

Marilyn, don't let the
windbags put you to sleep.
And yes, I just love this
idea of e-mailing each other
stories. I am proud to be a
member of *Row Man.CITY*,
aren't you?
    - Cath

A Night
in Soho
with
Catherine
the Great

I PUSHED my fifty-year-old boobs in the faces of those three little princesses who told me I was too experienced for him.

They backed off—he came close.

He was my emperor of the night—my palomino king—ring-a-ding-ding.

I watched as he galloped round and round some sculpture thing in the park.

We walked to that bar in Soho where he trembled in the draft by the window, the street light falling on his golden lengths. My crown wobbled as I leaned my head against him.

He sighed, long and shivery.

"They'll be here any time now," I whispered.

He made the sweetest whistling sound then.

A moment later the handlers arrived.

In the excitement, he lost his balance and lay across me, neighing. His eyeballs rolled as one of my men helped him out the door of the bar.

"Next!" I smiled.

I heard his hoofs faintly chime on the cobbles.

It was just another one of those cool Soho nights.

(R)eply, (E)mail reply, follow
(T)hread, (P)revious or (N)ext n

```
*Row Man.CITY*
Msg #10000
From: John Wayne's last lover
To: Catherine the Great
Subj: ERECTIONS
```

```
Catherine, you should try a
real man.
   - John Wayne's last lover
```

John Wayne
at the
Chelsea
Hotel

JOHN WAYNE took off his cowboy chaps and lay down on my bed at the Chelsea Hotel.

"Shall I tie you up and rape you?" I said.

"A woman can't rape a man," he laughed. "I wouldn't get an erection."

"Yes, John, you would," I said. "It happens."

And then I lay down on top of him, as if I had sex like this every day, and when I reached over and hand-cuffed his wrists, he didn't object. I felt very pretty and powerful too, because he was giving in to a girl like me.

And then—there it was, pointing west to the Hudson. I touched its pink nose and made a cooing sound as if I was talking to a baby.

"I can do some things," I said and then I did them.

Nothing changed.

I let out the most god-awful whimper and curled into a ball.

"I'm so sorry," I said. "Will you forgive me?"

(R)eply, (E)mail reply, follow
(T)hread, (P)revious or (N)ext n

```
*Row Man.CITY*
Msg #21986
From: Helen of Troy
To: All Greeks
Subj: NEANDERTHAL GUYS



The world is full of
Neanderthal guys, as far
as I'm concerned.
    - Helen
```

I'm Helen of Troy, I Am

I'M BACK HOME in Sparta and nothing has changed. My ex, the king of Sparta, pours me a gin and tonic. He is still the same old Menelaus, throwing the extra lemon peels down his dazzling marble sink and turning on his garburator.

Then he orders me and my daughter, Hermione, out to the garden so we can watch him pull his triple-jet sprinkler around his newly sodded backyard.

"Tell me you'll never leave me," Menelaus liked to say. Then he left to play with something or other.

So I went off with the prince of Troy. What have Menelaus and I learned after all those years apart?

I have learned the Trojan War had nothing to do

with me or my love for Paris. It was just a bunch of out-of-work boys fighting over saving face.

You know what they say, don't you? A hundred lovers, a hundred projections, and not one of them is you.

As for Menelaus, if he had it to do over, he'd do it the same old way. Even after the fall of Troy, he continues to send our weak male children to die in the mountains and takes the strong ones for his army. He refuses to erect walls around our kingdom. And he still brags that he trusts in the strength of soldiers.

"When you're happy and you know it, clap your hands," my daughter Hermione sings. I clap my hands, so does she.

Should I make her happy and go back to her father? Can I start over?

Can the face that launched a thousand ships put on her old red nightie and sleep-walk back into the Mycenaean time zone?

In a twinkling, I see my ex fire up our old gas barbecue and throw on a carcass of mutton.

When you're happy and you know it—clap your hands—

"Tell me you'll never leave me," Menelaus whispers

as I walk towards him, smiling and clapping. He is waiting, his feet planted on his freshly sodded backyard. Beyond his head, the hose jets sprinkle rainbow water.

```
(R)eply, (E)mail reply, follow
(T)hread, (P)revious or (N)ext n
```

```
*Row Man.City*
Msg #22342
From: The Great Hannibal
To: Slave Girls Everywhere
Subj: NEANDERTHAL GUYS




    No woman will ever
    understand the pressures we
    men face.
        - Hannibal
```

I, Hannibal, Experience Feelings No Warrior Should Have

F OR ME, Hannibal, the African hero, you wanted
to be wet like water—what could be more basic?
Wet like milk and seaweed and ocean surf. Wet
like the fizzy mist of fountains and silky June rain—
And—oh, my dear.
It was not a good plan.

You saw me cockeyed from the start. A wizard on an elephant, riding into the Alps. And you, the slave girl on my lap, making me catch my breath under our coat of bear skin.

All around me, my men were falling over precipices. My elephants shook from the cold even though I covered the hapless creatures with tent flaps. I lost an eye. And packhorses too—over the cliffs. We were ambushed, we survived an avalanche. You were with me. Even so, I can't begin to tell you how we suffered.

As time went on, the campaigns grew harder. You told me to go forward to Rome—after my great victory at Cannae. I had the Italians in my palm. I was losing your favour. You said I liked war, not winning. Where was the wizard on his elephant? The giant who trembled beneath your little hand?

Before your eyes, I turned into a troll scuttling across the battlefields. I became a one-eyed gnome in your bed. Limp and—worse—wizened, white, like a slightly hairy old root.

You felt as if you had found me under a leaf some place in Sicily. On our way home to Carthage, you said I could still draw you in. Even as a grub, I had my charms.

In exile, I experienced feelings no warrior should have. So I took the poison and died. Because you said: "Hannibal, this is your greatest trick of all. You have changed shapes so many times, I can no longer see you. I guess you are a wizard, after all."

(R)eply, (E)mail reply, follow
(T)hread, (P)revious or (N)ext n

het–

Row Man.CITY
Msg #323232
From: Gertrude Stein
To: Romance City
Subj: HETEROCENTRICTY

erocen–

You hets and your gender
skirmishes. Here or, rather,
there, there.
    – Gertrude

tricity

No Doubt
You Have
Forgotten Our
Night at
the Carlyle

(for Alice B. Toklas)

N O DOUBT you have forgotten our night at the Carlyle. The conversation had turned to sex, and then to death—the way it often does, in our strange age.

The unhappy movie star was there and two diesel-dykes with cameras and you wanted to confess everything.

You said you thought of a female body every time your husband made you come. You told me this after deliberating for several minutes about whether you wanted to tell me the worst thing you had ever done.

No, that wasn't the confession you started to tell me. Just the one you thought up to get out of telling me the truly terrible thing that was on your mind. Now that you thought of it, you said, it was so awful and unspeakable that you would never tell anyone.

Meanwhile, in the lobby of the Carlyle Hotel, the two photographers were chasing the high-chested movie star again.

"Mia, honey. Give us a photo! Come back, Mia! Give us a shot!" the photographers yelled and you and I stopped eating our cashews and drinking our cranberry cocktails and turned to see the two women run for the second time after the movie star who fled past us, sighing and tossing her head.

I can say this now — after I left you so abruptly.

(R)eply, (E)mail reply, follow
(T)hread, (P)revious or (N)ext n

```
*Row Man.CITY*
Msg #666666
From: Andrew's girlfriend
To: Andrew Dice Clay
Subj: DOGS
```

dogs

```
Gertrude's right. I just
wish my mom understood
my guy.
    - Andrew's girlfriend
```

Andrew Dogman

M Y MOTHER had gone to a lot of trouble the other night, Andrew. She brought in the drinks on a silver tray, the way she always does. And she looked so pretty in her old Halston suit. It just broke my heart that we didn't have a better time. What you did was unfortunate. I know dogs can't help themselves. It's pure instinct with you. I told Mom there was no reason to take it personally. After all, I managed to pry you off—finally. She didn't like that humping motion you make either. It's so—literal. I know—I shouldn't have smacked you on the nose. Dogs have feelings too. I felt bad the moment I saw you start to crawl under her sideboard.

I told Mom sometimes you require a bit of patience. You have so many insecurities. Yes, you do get carried away. With sniffing—and licking—down there—and I have to pat your head and say your name quite sharply: "Andrew Dogman! Stop that!" And then the sucking noises will stop.

```
(R)eply, (E)mail reply, follow
(T)hread, (P)revious or (N)ext n
```

```
*Row Man.CITY*
Msg #Buckingham Palace
From: Queen Elizabeth
To: All
Subj: TENNIS
```

tennis

I realize this is the
community we all have been
searching for. A place where
people must be judged by
their thoughts and hopes,
instead of how they look. But
I see no reason why someone
like Andrew Dice Clay and his
girlfriend should be allowed
in *Row Man.CITY*. Surely,
we have some standards!
  - Liz

Game:
Love = Love

_____

(for Princess Di)

MY DAUGHTER-IN-LAW and the tennis pro are hard at it. I am hard at it, too.

The imperious young man stands on the other side of the net, crashing balls at us.

Princess Di cries and stomps when she misses his serve and I have to send it back.

But every time I hit the ball, my poor dogs howl. They want me to throw it to them.

My doggy dogs are the only ones who don't think of me as sovereign of the realm. They are waiting for me to finish our set so I can put on my Wellies and run with them through the wet grass. We like the rain, my dawgie-wawgies and I.

Prince Philip sits with them as my daughter-in-law and I go at it pell-mell. He knows we are fighting for our lives. My dogs know nothing of the sort. They don't care if Princess Di pivots around and around on her faithless foot.

It's me their little pop-out eyes watch. Now and always.

That is the only real order left.

I stand at the net and drill another ball down the court.

```
(R)eply, (E)mail reply, follow
(T)hread, (P)revious or (N)ext n
```

re-

Row Man.CITY
Msg #38888
From: Newt Gingrich
To: Those of you with blue eyes
Subj: REPENTANCE

pen-

tance

To Those
of You
with
Blue Eyes

———————

Dear ——:
I am sending this letter to all the women who have been
in my life because what I have to say makes general ob-
servations about my experiences with each of you.

I want you to realize I am aware there could be some
improvements in my own conduct.

Here is an example of my behaviour which comes to
mind: my promises, guarantees and my vows were not always kept. I often created a world for us in charming, well-
spoken words—hollow words.

Today, I know that if one isn't honest with oneself, as well as with others, then one will never be able to find the smooth road. As you may not realize, things have not always been easy for me.

But the reasons for my hardships are not the important consideration here. These reasons are for me to understand. What *is* important is that I acknowledge what I have done to you so that you and I can move closer.

As I write you, I do not feel self-pity, guilt or shame. I feel sobered, but also glad, not just for you but for myself. This has been a long time coming. Although life may not have the glow it once had for you, at the same time, I hope it has never felt better.

Am I asking for forgiveness? I think that is for you to decide.

I am still very close to most of you, and for those whom I am not close to, I hope we can heal what it is that keeps us at a distance.

I ask you not to discuss this letter with anyone and that this remain a private correspondence between us.

If you want to write me regarding this matter, please address all correspondence to the United States Congress, Washington.

Finally, I ask you to accept my apology for how I have hurt and disappointed you. I hope I didn't ruin your life.

love, Newt

(It is a great pleasure to bring
this e-mailing to a close. If
you have stories dealing with
integrity and reformation of
character, please e-mail:
<*Fam.Ly.VALUES*@web.sh.ss.org>.)

(R)eply, (E)mail reply, follow
(T)hread, (P)revious or (N)ext n

```
*Row Man.CITY*
Msg #31234
From: Ufila, Goth girl
To: Newt
Subj: WIMPS
```

##**! Newt! Don't be such a wimp! We're not stopping now. This is my tale! Take it to heart!
  - Goth girl

The Days
of Barbarian
Love

GETTING RAPED was over before I knew it, but I want
to tell you about getting murdered first.

I was living near the river Tisza in Hungary, when
both such unfortunate circumstances occurred.

The year was A.D. 453—a very good year for Attila who
was busy conquering the world. And for me, Ufila, the
Goth girl whose name is a contraction for Little Wolf.

Getting murdered

I was standing at the door of Attila's tent.

"Attila? Are you here?" I called. The hall of his

magnificent tent was in darkness and, for once, free of cooking smells.

No answer.

Oh, well.

I went in.

In those days, we just walked in and out of each other's tents without being invited. An old barbarian custom.

Beyond the first hall, I saw a figure hiding behind a screen of silk. Gold and precious ornaments shone on its head. If I didn't know the plain ways of my Attila, I would have thought it was the Scourge of God himself.

"Who are you?" I called. "Show me your face."

Berichos the Scythian, my ex-lover, stepped out from behind the screen.

"Your bridegroom couldn't make it," he said.

Berichos smiled a smile of barbarian love.

"And now I'm going to kill you!" Berichos produced a sword and began to lurch unsteadily towards me.

A Hun is so used to riding, he is sometimes less than sure-footed.

It is said Attila himself learned to ride before he could walk, and that he performs all his bodily functions on horseback.

Only Attila was nowhere to be seen.

"Berichos, why?"

Zip—his sword whistled by my ear.

"As if you don't know!"

For the first time, I saw my body—without the soul-spirit of Ufila—yes, I saw my Goth-girl body laid bare on Attila's floor and Huns standing over it, talking Hunnish.

I fell on a couch. The vulnerability of my own flesh was a secret my mother had kept from me.

"Prepare to die, Ufila!"

I held out my arm to Berichos, smiling like Saint Genevieve when she persuaded Attila not to torch Paris.

"Berichos, Attila has been seating you two seats to his left." Patiently, I kept my arm upstretched. I had all of barbarian goodness on my side.

"You're just sick of him treating you as second rank. And I don't blame you."

"I love you!" Berichos wailed as he placed his sword tip on my heart.

"Berichos." I curled my fingers around his weapon until I smelled a smell like copper and I knew the smell belonged to me. *"Give it over!"*

"Ah, Ufila—you are always the strong one. That's why I love you."

With a clank, his bloodied sword fell at my feet.

Berichos sat down at a table. I hadn't noticed this before, but it was set for two. A rose drooped from one of those old mead bottles which were very popular circa 450—the days of barbarian love.

Berichos threw down some cooked mutton.

"Lunch, Ufila?"

"You bet." I wiped my bloody hand on my sheepskin shirt and fell to gorging.

Getting raped

Getting raped is a shorter story. It happened later the same day when I let Onegesios, Attila's right-hand man, walk me back to my tent.

Now, how did getting raped go? It went like this.

I felt relaxed because I wasn't expecting it, so I bounced off my tent like it was a trampoline. And came back laughing.

"A woman like you has to learn," he said and lunged again.

"Learn what, Onegesios?" I shrieked.

"How to please a man," Onegesios said. "How to look after him, Little Wolf." And Onegesios threw me on the floor.

All because I drank from the mead bowl first.

"You should have waited until I drank some," Onegesios yelled. He crouched over me, his hands around my throat.

All because he wanted the mead first! I screamed with laughter. It was the craziest thing I ever heard.

Then came the moment when I did not laugh — the moment when I knew this barbarian was stronger than me!

At that same moment, Attila stepped into my tent. He was not dressed like Onegesios, or even Berichos. No Indian pearls, no silks from Phoenicia — nothing but simple ivy-wood bowls, and common ponies for my Attila.

"Enjoying yourself, Ufila?" Attila said as he threw Onegesios out of my tent.

"My love, it's not what you think." I spoke in a bright, conversational tone, as if I was drinking cherry juice with the Roman consul.

"I'll teach you to lie!" Attila hit me with his unjewelled fist.

Attila, my darling, my dearest one, in whose eyes I saw the loneliness of a woman unable to speak her pain. He died some days later in my arms, bleeding through the nose.

We are all barbarians here.

```
(R)eply, (E)mail reply, follow
(T)hread, (P)revious or (N)ext n
```

```
*Row Man.CITY*
Msg #000009
From: The Boston Strangler
To: Ufila, Goth girl
Subj: STAB
```

stab

```
Ufila, you wouldn't have got
away with murder if you were
my girl.
   - Albert Henry DeSalvo
```

East River Fantasy

GLIDING DOWN the shore of the East River, you began to think the driver of the yellow cab was me.

You kept on looking at him, and by and by, you were sure it was me, sitting up in the front seat, like a nice East Coast cabby, driving so nicely, nice hands on the wheel, humming so nicely to the radio playing "Wild Horses."

All you had to do was close your eyes and loop the loop down the East River into my arms.

Across the water, Riker's Island Penitentiary sat in the middle of a bunch of trees.

"I want to get out right here," you said.

The cabby slammed on the brakes.

"Women like you drive me nuts."

Not one to pass up a challenge, you got out of the cab.

And there I was—under the bridge. You were only a few minutes late.

```
(R)eply, (E)mail reply, follow
(T)hread, (P)revious or (N)ext n
```

cen-

Row Man.CITY
Msg #444444
From: A Roman Polanski admirer
To: Queen Elizabeth
Subj: CENSORSHIP

sor-

Liz, we can't kick out Andrew
Dice Clay or, for that
matter, the Boston
Strangler! The World Wide
Web is open to everyone.
   - A Roman Polanski admirer

ship

I Had No Intention of Kidnapping a Harmless Delivery Man

(for Roman Polanski)

JUST SO YOU CAN SEE I had no intention of kidnapping a harmless delivery man—let me tell you about the innocent way that evening began.
I was alone, getting ready to write.

I was in that anxious, prewriting state when any distraction looks more promising than the work at hand.

And my mood was as flat as an antediluvian seabed where ancient female souls awaited some awful primordial doom.

Uh-huh, I was premenstrual too.

As I stared through my window, the lights winked out on the Empire State building.

And then I heard the thing no New Yorker wants to hear. An unexpected knock. After midnight.

I peered, trembling, through the tiny porthole of my dooroscope.

"Who's there?"

A voice with an accent I didn't recognize, and what's worse, a slurred voice, a drunken voice, said it was the pizza man. The pizza man, my foot. I peered through my peephole and found myself staring at a cleft chin. That chin showed, I thought, a feminine desire to be loved, and those coquettish lips—so very female, don't you think? They revealed an immense desire for appreciation. People with lips like that want to show their family and friends they amount to something.

I thought I'd rearrange his features a little. Give him a high, wide forehead . . . a long, wide nose—the sign of positive energy—thin out the curves on his upper lip but still keep his mouth full . . .

"What's in the box?" I asked.

"The whole enchilada," he laughed and flipped up the lid. Sure enough, I saw a giant pizza. It dripped with honey-coloured cheese. It was Sicilian pizza, my favourite. How could I resist?

It's Christmas now

It's Christmas now. The Metropolitan Life Insurance Building is a sumptuous sheath of red and green light. I still write long hours into the night on my assignments but my darling never complains from his place on the floor. I can't say I feel sorry for him because he's used to being tied up and tormented. The poor thing likes it. And I remind him when he gets discouraged that I do like to take him to a lot of parties.

```
(R)eply, (E)mail reply, follow
(T)hread, (P)revious or (N)ext n
```

freedom

of

speech

Row Man.CITY
Msg #44445
From: A Roman Polanski admirer
To: All
Subj: FREEDOM OF SPEECH

I Dreamt I Ate the Testicles of the Celebrated Young Author Who Writes So Lovingly about Cruelty to Women

(for Bret Easton Ellis)

I DREAMT I ate the testicles of the celebrated young author who writes so lovingly about cruelty to women.

I ate them, just weeks ago, in the Casa Di Pré, with some linguine in white clam sauce.

As I ate the testicles of the young author, I thought about the last time I'd seen him. On the jacket of a book, of course. He was sitting backwards and astride a chair, looking very sorry for himself. It was all he could do to contain his self-pity as he arranged himself in the pose the photographer suggested.

I didn't eat any of the big, shiny red tulips on the restaurant windowsill. After all, it was April. I was in Greenwich Village. Only the bricked street looked like Paris and the sky was glowing wild and winter dark.

The woman at the next table went outside for a look.

"Is it snowing?" I asked when she came back.

"No," she said and sat back down at her table whose pink cloth was the exact same colour as the sugar packages of Sweet 'n Low.

"That white stuff we are seeing is various debris."

Just then a red Coca-Cola truck splashed past the window.

It was a ravishing moment, I can tell you. The really red, wet truck, the spring flowers, the various debris, and me chewing what I was chewing and chewing.

(R)eply, (E)mail reply, follow
(T)hread, (P)revious or (N)ext n

```
*Row Man.CITY*
Msg #35486
From: Anonymous
To: All
Subj: FICTIONS
```

fictions

```
Here's one you probably
heard before.
    - Anonymous
```

The Age of Ambivalent Men

(for Marco Polo, Casanova and Rimbaud)

THAT'S the kind of age it was. So there.

"Marco's a roamer, hon," Mrs. Polo sighed. "You must know what he's like by now."

We were standing on a balcony in the Rialto, watching the Polo galley sail out of the Grand Canal towards the melancholy horizon. Uncle Maffeo and his father Niccolo were on board, but not Mrs. Polo or me.

Five stories below, near the muddy olive waters, slavers were shutting up their stalls, and men on the moored barges were screaming and waving their arms. It was raining. It is almost always raining in Venice.

My mother-in-law pressed a piece of stone in my hand. "Before the Piazza San Marco was paved, I found this," she told me. "That was over fifteen years ago, which is exactly how long I had to wait for my husband to come back. May you not have to wait so long!"

Then she threw up her hands, kissed me and left. She was on her way to market, and I was on my way to a lifetime of letter writing.

I didn't mind. I knew Marco was the man for me. I never went through problems of marital adjustment. When I felt lonely, I invented scenes of domestic joy. I projected all my best qualities on my husband, who gave me space—and scope.

A man out of reach asks little, and he will be who-ever you want him to be.

Naturally, I received letters about the Khan and the way he doted on my young, credulous Marco. I had to skip over the parts about the swanky battles, the Mon-gols' snow-white cattle, their printing block books, their silly tents made of canes.

I was proud, though, when Marco was made gover-nor of the city of Yangchow. I told everyone he would be home soon, when I knew it would be another decade at least before I saw his kind, lion eyes.

Yes, I read *The Travels of Marco Polo* years before he wrote it.

A few centuries later I met Casanova. He wasn't sailing off to the Orient, oh no, not him. He was hurrying across the Bridge of Sighs on his way to prison.

I brought Giovanni Giacomo Casanova his meals every day in his four-by-four cell under the roof of the doge's palace, and I stuck in a tankard for the jailor too.

I knew he'd never tell anyone how I disguised myself as a boy and tied my gondola up to a statue in the flooded Piazza San Marco. I began to shake when I saw the head and shoulders of my long-legged vagabond break through the prison's lead roof. There was so much moonlight.

"You are my romantic ideal," Casanova said and we kissed a kiss he will never forget. Then I poled him safe and sound to Mestre, and out of my life.

Why should I resent Giovanni for setting me free? Who could ask for anything more?

As the millennium drew to a close, I met a sulky nineteen-year-old—the only one in the Age of Ambivalent Men who wasn't Venetian. Arthur Rimbaud believed poetry was going to overturn the social order.

My sentiments exactly.

Of course, there were difficulties: Arthur's big hair (he wore it long and hated to wash it), and his manners in bed.

"A writer like you ought to talk dirty better," he told me the first time we slid between the sheets. We were holed up in a farmhouse I'd rented in Belgium. I'd managed to get him away from his mother and the other bad influences in his life, like Verlaine.

"Where's your erotic language!" he screamed. "Your vocabulary needs work!"

All I said was, "I want you."

In English.

Soon there were no more little upsets because Arthur went off to sell guns in the Middle East. It turns out he was mad at literature, not me.

I loved him best when he was doing construction work in Cyprus. Or looking for ivory in Harar. While he was away, I spent hours imagining how good he and I could be together. I saw us in later years as authors on world book tours, talking about the way love had transformed our lives.

If only he would come back so we could start again.

My dear, joyless, judgemental and ill-kempt Rimbaud. He knew that to wait is to create.

And then the worst thing happened. Arthur came back. I heard the news from his mother who went to see him in the hospital at Marseilles. He lost his leg and they both wrote, begging me to join them, but by then it was too late.

A new millennium was beginning, and I didn't want to miss out.

(R)eply, (E)mail reply, follow
(T)hread, (P)revious or (N)ext n

```
*Row Man.CITY*
Msg #333302
From: Young working girl
To: All
Subj: FETISHES
```

fetishes

```
Howard says he doesn't care
who comes to *Row Man.CITY*,
as long as he can stay where
he is.
   - Young working girl
```

I Catch Flies for the Richest Man in the World

(for Howard Hughes)

I CATCH FLIES for the richest man in the world. He is not dead but holed up in a suite at the top of the Empire State Building. Germ-free, of course.

From our windows, you can see the polar bear in Central Park.

And the flagpole they built for the old airships.

It always makes me a little self-conscious saying "The Empire State" to cab drivers. Sometimes I just say "Fifth Avenue and Thirty-fourth," or "I'll tell you where to stop."

I do not go out; I do not see anyone.

In the morning, I call up Rexall Drugs. I tell them I need more Kimberly-Clark facial tissue and Life Brand paper towels.

As everybody knows, the richest man in the world has to blow his nose.

If Rexall Drugs say they're fresh out, I call up Wal-Mart. A delivery boy brings up the stuff in the secret elevator.

Then I put on a floor-length white operating gown and long white gloves. Taking small steps, I enter the bedroom of the richest man in the world. I do not talk or make rustling sounds.

When I get to within three feet of him, I replace the lining of paper towels on the floor. I sit down on the bed beside him, making certain I do not disturb the paper towels under us.

I turn on the VCR. And stick in some old films— *Myra Breckinridge*, *Strange Bedfellows*, *Executive Suite*, *Evel Knievel* and *Gone with the Wind*. If he and I concentrate, we can usually get through five by supper.

And I catch flies without squashing them.

How can I catch a fly without squashing it? I wait for the fly to land on my left palm. The fly must face me. Then I move my cupped right hand very slowly towards my left palm. I tap my left palm and the little thing flies right into the heel of my cupped palm.

Naturally, I have to move my gloved hand at the speed of sixty feet a second and calculate for a slight overshoot.

I insert the fly into a vacuum air chute at my feet. I do not tell him how many I catch.

When it's over, I fetch a small basin of warm water. And some pHisoHex soap. I wash off my almost-fly-walked-on hands.

And I take off my clothes and proceed to wash myself all over with Sunlight soap.

He just lies there, propped up and staring.

I must not make even a ripple on the paper towels.

```
(R)eply, (E)mail reply, follow
(T)hread, (P)revious or (N)ext n
```

Row Man.CITY
Msg #77799
From: The author
To: *Row Man.CITY*
Subj: PERFECT GUYS

perfect

I can't help having the last
word. Here's a story that
might interest you.
    - the author

guys

The
Man Doll

————————

I MADE the doll for Helen.

I wanted to build a surrogate toy that would satisfy my friend so completely I would never have to listen to her litany of grievances against the male sex again.

My name is Aphrid. I am a retired bio-medical engineer on the planet Astarte. When I made the doll in the summer of 2103, I was eighty-one and Helen was eighty-nine. On my modest pension, I couldn't afford to buy Helen one of the million-dollar symbiotes called Pleasure Boys, which the wealthy women and gay men purchase in our exclusive department stores.

I didn't like these display models anyhow. Their platinum hair and powder-blue eyes (identical colouring of Pleasure Girls) looked too artificial, and I'd heard complaints about their emotional range. The human interface on these male dolls was limited to one expression: a pleased, slightly predatory smile to indicate sexual interest. I wanted a new prototype that every woman would love to own—a deluxe model that combined the virility component of a human male with full nurture capability. In short, I wanted a Pleasure Boy whose programming emphasized the ability to put your needs ahead of his own.

I made my doll at home, requisitioning extra limbs or organs from the Cosmetic Clinic in Facial Repairs where I used to work. My former job made it easy for me to find my pick of anatomical bargains. I particularly liked the selection of machine extensions offered by the Space Force Bank. After careful consideration, I chose long, sinewy hands, arms and legs, and made sure they were the type that could be willed into action in a twinkling. The Space Force Bank simulated the doll's computer brain from mine for $1,500.

At her age, Helen said it was high time she gave up relationships, but I was sure she still craved love and affection. So I gave the doll a plastic exterior that felt lifelike to the touch, and made sure its interface could display six basic emotions: anger, disgust, fear, surprise, sadness and happiness. After all, a machine that communicates emotional information reduces stress on the user and I wanted Helen to have nothing but the best.

I also placed a nuclear reactor the size of a baseball in the chest cavity, just where the heart is in the human body. The reactor warmed the doll by transmitting heat to a labyrinth of coils. The reactor uses a caesium source that yields an 80 per cent efficiency rate, with a life expectancy of just over thirty years. The doll was activated by a hand-held switch.

Each night in my flat I worked on the doll with my arthritic hands. Most of my finger joints are swollen and some of my fingers no longer move at all, but the thought of Helen's pleasure kept me going.

I wanted the doll to be a perfect human likeness, so exact in detail that nobody would guess Helen's escort was a robot. For the final touches, I shaped its interface with the help of liquid silicone and I applied synthetic hair transplants without a hitch. My savings had almost run out by the time I got to the sex organs, but luckily I was able to find a cheap set from a secondhand supplier. For $250 I bought an antique organ that belonged to a fifty-year-old Pleasure Boy. I hoped its primitive hydraulic system would work under stress.

The laws on Astarte forbid symbiotes to waste human food. So I built in a silicone oesophagus and a crude bladder because I wanted the doll to have something to do on social occasions. These tubes allowed the doll to ingest and pass out water-and-sugar solution. Of course, it didn't defecate. The doll's nuclear waste products were internally controlled and required changing once every ten years.

At the last moment I realized I'd forgotten to add dye to the pupils, so its eyes were almost colourless. But in all other aspects, my doll looked normal.

When I installed its reactor, the doll came to life, lolling contentedly in my apartment, ignoring the discomfort of its mummy case and its helmet of elastic bandages and gauze. The doll called me Aphrid in a friendly baritone, and, despite its post-operative daze, began to display a talent for understanding and devotion.

It could sense when I felt sad and sighed sympathetically. If I was angry or frustrated, the doll didn't try to argue me out of my feelings, but murmured behind its bandages: "I know just how you feel."

When I came home, the doll would be waiting for me, ready to serve dinner.

"Welcome home, Aphrid!" the doll would cry. "How gorgeous you look!"

At first, I had to stop myself from disagreeing when the doll made its flattering remarks.

"You shouldn't use the word 'gorgeous'," I'd tell the doll as we sat down to our meal. "It's not appropriate for a woman my age."

"Why not, Aphrid?" my doll murmured. "What could be better than a body which is essentially characterized."

"Pardon?" I said. (I'd given the doll a rather large vocabulary.)

"Your body has real character," the doll said. "Look at me. I am plain unvarnished plastic."

"You still look very nice," I said, surprised to find myself reassuring the doll.

"But you look as if you have lived," the doll said. "And I find that irresistible." Then he would stroke my arm as if he meant it.

At the end of five months, I removed its protective case and found myself staring at a nice-looking robot whose pale, all-forgiving eyes gazed back at me with love. The doll's most distinctive feature (aside from its strange eyes) was the wild bush of dark hair that corkscrewed back from its forehead. (I had matched the doll's hair type to mine—when I'd been a great deal younger.)

My desire to give the doll to Helen suddenly vanished.

I decided to keep my creation.

I called it Manny.

Soon, I was unable to keep my hands off him. The first night we made love I had a case of nerves. The doll was used to the way the top half of me looks. I mean the way I appear to be wearing someone else's head on my shoulders. (I have spent my old salary on numerous face lifts, but don't have the cash to fix my neck where the skin gathers in folds like finely wrinkled silk.) So I worried that Manny would be revolted by what lies under my clothes. Because if truth is to be found, it isn't in my aging buttocks, or my breasts and torso, which are peppered with telling brown spots. Why did I build such a youthful toy, I wondered, when I could have made a doll who looked my age? Anxiously, I started mixing up some martinis. The doll watched me closely. He wasn't used to seeing me do something for him.

"Manny, here's to us!" I handed him his glass. I figured a little Vermouth and gin wouldn't hurt the doll's silicone oesphagus. Then I turned down the lights.

Manny sipped his drink and smiled, and I smiled back, suddenly embarrassed. Was I going to have to stage manage the whole thing? I shrugged and put down my glass. Why not? I was hardly unexperienced. I stood close to the robot.

"Manny," I whispered. "Hold me."

My doll slid his arm around my waist and then froze.

"Aphrid? Haven't we forgotten something?" the doll murmured.

"Have we?" I said.

The doll nodded and disappeared into his bedroom. He came out carrying one of my small shoe boxes. He opened it. Inside the box, I saw an array of artificial penises—everything from a latex vibrator in electric blue to a silicone dildo in a wide range of colours.

"Please choose," the doll said.

I'd forgotten I'd made twenty different types of penises for Manny, thinking Helen would enjoy trying them out.

"Aphrid?" the doll said. He sounded impatient.

I selected the latex in electric blue and Manny stepped out of his pants and hung them neatly on a chair. Then he turned his back to me and began unscrewing his homemade prothesis. He seemed to be having trouble, and I felt a harrowing sympathy for my doll. I, too, feel put together. I wanted to rush over and help, but something in the way Manny was standing told me to wait. At last, my doll turned round. He was grinning and his shocking blue penis was buzzing faintly.

l started to giggle.

"Come here, Aphrid," the doll said and I did.

Everything operated above normal capacity, thanks to Manny's hydraulic accumulator which supplied intense power for short periods of time. But it wasn't Manny's vibrating penis that pleased me most. The sturdy vinyl of Manny's lingual muscles made oral sex with my doll simply sensational. For the first time in my life I understood the term 'multiple orgasms'.

Naturally, my doll didn't ejaculate although it was clever at making satisfied groans and noises for my benefit. On Astarte, it is illegal for a doll to create life. The sole function of a symbiote is recreational.

The next few months with Manny were a miracle. To my surprise, I felt the swelling caused by my arthritis recede and I began to go out on a regular basis. I dressed in sunny colours and wore scarfs around my neck. With Manny's help, I installed an aviary of doves in our apartment. We planted pots of jasmine on the balcony outside our window and at night I would lie in bed with

Manny and smell its mysterious and lovely scent. In the mornings, I began to rise at six as if the day ahead was a mythic adventure I could shape to my wishes. Affectionately, the doll sometimes called me by the archaic Earth version of my name—Aphrodite.

When my joints didn't ache, there was nothing physical I wouldn't try. Sunrise meditations, chanting and milk baths with Manny who seemed to revel in the happy feelings I had about myself. The doll's appreciation of my body had changed me. This is what our bodies are for, I realized. It was unnatural to think we had to stay frozen in one stage in order to be loved.

But after almost a year with Manny, I began to feel uncomfortable about creating a robot whose life was built around ministering to my needs. I wasn't used to having somebody serve me. As a woman on Astarte, I'd been brought up to serve others. Even in my former profession, I'd still been taking care of people. I grew sullen and impatient and found myself resenting the doll's presence. I started to think I'd overdone its mellifluous baritone, which sounded theatrical and false to me now. Then my former employer asked me to come out of retirement and teach the young interns at the Clinic. So once again I began to spend my days at work and in the evenings, I visited with old friends, including Helen who quizzed me about my personal life. I told her I was living with somebody, but said nothing about Manny being a robot.

One night, just before bedtime, the doll didn't bring in the platter of fruit and hot cocoa I'd come to expect. Instead it sank down on our bed, its silicone interface sagging.

"Aphrid, I don't know what's the matter with me," the doll sighed. Tears began to leak from its colourless eyes.

"Maybe you are bored with looking after me," I said.

"No, no," Manny sighed. "It's just that you eat out with your friends and never bring them home to visit. Don't you need me any more?"

"Of course I do," I said. "Maybe the time has come for us to do a little entertaining."

"Oh, thank you, Aphrid! There's nothing I'd like better!" The doll stopped crying and began to smile lovingly once more.

Even though I felt bored with my homelife, I still felt a thrill when Helen shuffled into my living room and stared at Manny in frank sexual admiration. My doll did look handsome. He wore a pair of designer jeans and a tight-fitting T-shirt and his synthetic head was bent as he placed a dish on the table so Helen couldn't see his eyes.

Not that Helen would catch on to Manny's flaws easily. Helen has what our doctor calls 'floaters,' the small spots that coast across your pupils, partially obscuring vision. She also has gout in her ankles and feet. Which was why she was carrying a walking stick that evening. (Sadly enough, although our protein rich diets can prolong human life to well over a hundred, nobody on Astarte has found a cure for such minor ailments.)

"Don't tell me this sexy young man is living with you!" Helen said in her flat-footed way.

Most people find Helen a bit hard to take, but I have always forgiven her gaffes. My father once told me that keeping old friends is a sign of good character. And I suppose that is what Helen is to me—first and foremost, my best character reference. Nobody else knows me as long or as well.

"Everybody says I look like Aphrid," the doll piped up as it bustled about, pouring our drinks.

"There is a slight resemblance." Helen collapsed onto the sofa beside me. "What are doing with somebody twice your age?"

"Forty times you mean," the doll said proudly. "I am—well, quite new."

Helen peered up at the doll.

"Young man, come here a minute," she said.

Manny bent down so Helen could see his face. She started to shriek.

"You're a doll!" she cried.

"Yes," Manny said, grinning.

Helen turned to me.

"You're living with a doll!"

I nodded. "Not just *a* doll. *My* doll. I made Manny." I blushed. "Actually, I made him for you and then I decided to keep him for myself."

"You don't mean you have sex with it!" Helen poked my leg with her walking sticking. She was laughing very hard. "At your age!"

"What's wrong with my age?" I said huffily. "Surely, you don't believe our desires fade away entirely."

"Don't they?" Helen said. She stared at me curiously.

"Of course not," I replied. "You should learn that our behaviour doesn't really depend on our age."

Helen looked thoughtful. "Aphrid, I read that our sexuality stops after menopause."

"All lies," I said. "Isn't it, Manny?"

"I think Helen is being coy with us," the doll replied.

"Nobody wants an old broad like me now." Helen began to play with the handle of her walking stick. "And I have nobody to blame but myself. I'm always shocked when I find out the people I love have feet of clay."

I saw Manny glance down at his new plastic feet. He was smiling in a way I hadn't seen for a long time.

"Maybe you should settle for a good machine," I said and winked at Manny.

I waited for Manny to wink back but the doll's colourless eyes didn't blink. In my rush to finish my creation, I'd forgotten to give him a sense of irony. Naturally, I'd programmed the doll to laugh at other people's jokes, but irony was a more complex skill and I hadn't wired it into Manny. It was only one of a few mistakes I was beginning to realize I'd made.

"There is love all around you, Helen." Manny reached over and interlocked his synthetic fingers with hers. "You just have to look."

"Oh, what do you know?" Helen grumbled. "You're only a robot!" She glared at Manny, daring him to argue back.

Of course, the doll's programming prohibited uncaring reactions. Manny knew Helen was distressed so he didn't take what she said personally. Yes, my doll was unique, not only among symbiotes, but among us humans. What person could love as unselfishly as my doll?

"Maybe I know more than you think," Manny said and then he did wink. "Ask Aphrid."

Helen giggled and so did Manny. Why did my doll sound so pleased? Manny, I thought, you'd be a lot less sympathetic if you knew Helen enjoyed feeling dissatisfied.

During dinner, Manny asked Helen about her seven marriages, and my friend talked eloquently about the effect of their emotional aftermath on her. When Manny refilled Helen's wineglass, I noticed the doll lightly brush her shoulder. Irritated, I stood up and cleared away the dishes. A few minutes later, Helen limped in.

"Thanks for having me over," Helen said. She coughed and stared at her walking stick. I waited.

"Would you mind..." Helen smirked.

"What?"

"You know."

"You want to have sex with my doll!"

Helen sighed. "You made him for me, didn't you?"

"No! Absolutely not!"

"Aphrid, Manny just asked if he could come home with me," Helen said.

"Don't be ridiculous!" I hurried out of the kitchen. Helen followed, her walking stick thumping.

In the living room, Manny was putting on his coat.

"Manny!" I said angrily. "What are you doing?"

"Goodbye, Aphrid," my doll said. "Helen needs me now."

Helen put on her coat too.

"Aphrid—don't be angry!" Helen said.

"Manny," I said. "You can't go—I own you."

"You don't mean that, Aphrid," Manny replied. "You know dolls have rights too."

"Who says? You can't procreate. You can't eat. And your retinas are colourless."

"It's just for a night or two," Helen cried.

"Helen—you—you stay out of this!" I nodded at my desk. "Manny, I'm warning you. If you go, I'll deactivate you."

My doll knew I kept his hand-held switch in one of the desk drawers.

"Aphrid, you're not the type of human to be petty," Manny replied.

"Oh yes I am."

As I started towards my desk, I saw Manny's interface shrink into an emotion I'd forgotten he could access. Disgust. He whispered something to Helen. She smiled at me sheepishly and hobbled out the door. Then Manny gently took my hand and sat me down on the sofa. I began to beg Manny not to go and the doll listened sympathetically, cocking his head and studying me with his colourless eyes, as if he was really considering the prospect of staying. But as the hours passed, I knew I'd been defeated. I'd made the doll for Helen and then decided to keep him for myself. Still, it didn't matter. My programming ensured that Manny would be drawn to whoever had most need of him.

When I awoke the next morning, the doll was gone. But true to his programming, Manny called later that day to see how I was doing. He told me I would be fine on my own so he was going to stay where he was. I slammed the phone down. At first, I felt angry with Helen for taking my doll. And then I began to regret the way I'd neglected Manny. I daydreamed about the activities he and I might have done together. Why hadn't we taken space holidays together, for instance? Or morphed ourselves on special occasions, like other couples, into mirror images of each other.

But soon I stopped feeling sad. In many ways, it was a relief not to have Manny underfoot, doing things for me that I had always liked to do myself. My arthritis was better and for the first time in ages, I could lounge about at home without anybody coming in to ask if I had everything I needed. A few weeks later, I took a short holiday.

The day I returned, there was a call from Helen. I put down my luggage, relieved to hear from my old friend.

"Aphrid, I'm sorry about what happened," Helen said.

"Look, you did me a favour. How's Manny?" I said.

"I'm worried about him," Helen said.

"Has something gone wrong with his programming?" I asked, feeling protective suddenly about my doll.

"Come for dinner and see for yourself."

I unpacked and headed for Helen's apartment. At the entrance to the building, I overheard three dolls talking to the doorman. One of the dolls, a Pleasure Girl with shoulder-length platinum hair, asked the doorman to let them in. The doorman shook his head.

"No dolls allowed in after six," the doorman said. "Astarte Towers is a respectable space block."

"We don't have to follow your rules." The female doll sauntered towards the entrance.

"Oh, yeah?" The doorman spun the doll around and punched her viciously in the chest. The doll groaned and tottered backwards. The male robot caught her and bent his head protectively towards the female doll who began making sad, little choking noises against his shoulder. The sight made me uneasy. There'd been reports of political rallies of dolls on television but I'd never observed them firsthand. The only symbiotes I'd seen in a group were unactivated models in store windows. I hurried past the miserable dolls and ran into the lobby.

In the small apartment, I found Manny putting an ice bucket on the drink tray. His silicone interface was set in an emotion I didn't recognize. Then he saw me.

"Aphrid! It's been too long!" the doll cried. "But you look wonderful! What have you been up to?"

"Taking care of myself," I smiled.

"Me too!" a voice called. It was Helen. I hadn't noticed her sitting in a rocker by the window. She glanced hungrily at Manny and then back at me.

"Uh-sorry, Aphrid," Helen mumbled. I shrugged. Why would I be jealous of somebody who had fallen for a pleasure toy—a high-wired batch of silicone and plastic!

"And how's the teaching job?" Manny asked.

I began to describe some research I was doing on a dish-face deformity. When I finished, I realized that Helen had been listening intently. Apparently, she had no interest in going into her usual grievances against the male sex. I felt a prickle of anger.

"Did you see any dolls at the door?" Helen asked.

"One or two," I admitted. "What are they doing here?"

"A few come every day. Sometimes humans come too. If they can get by the doorman, Manny lets them come in and talks to them," Helen groaned. "I suppose there's nothing wrong with the dolls getting political. Except I worry they tire Manny."

"Helen, I am tireless," Manny said, and I winced as I remembered just how tireless Manny could be.

Helen smiled dreamily. "Aphrid, I've never been in love like this."

"You said that about each of your husbands," I snapped.

"Okay, okay," Helen snorted. "But I don't think you understand. Manny and I are going to start a family."

"What?"

"Helen thinks my virility component can be rejigged for children," Manny said. "I've tried to tell her it's not possible, but she walks out of the room and refuses to listen." He sighed and for the first time I recognized Manny's odd expression. Frustration. I couldn't remember wiring that emotion into my doll.

"For once in my life I have the right partner," Helen giggled. "Just think of the wonderful children I would have with somebody like Manny."

"Well," Manny replied. "I could always talk it over with Aphrid."

"Isn't Manny sweet?" Helen said.

"Yes," I said, feeling suddenly envious. "Yes, he is. But haven't you forgotten something?"

Helen stared at me.

"It's against the law for dolls to procreate."

Helen stuck out her tongue and hobbled off to the kitchen.

"See?" Manny said. "That's what she always does."

Suddenly, a buzzer rang and the apartment door opened. The symbiotes I'd seen in the lobby crowded in.

"Pleasure Girl No. 024 found a way in through the back entrance," one of the male dolls cried. I slipped out to the kitchen where Helen stood pouring herself a drink.

The female doll didn't notice me. She kissed Manny on the cheek and my doll smiled for the first time that night.

"Pleasure Boy No. 025 suggested we try another door," she said. "Aren't we clever, for sex toys?" Suddenly, she pointed at me. "Manny! Who is that old woman with Helen?"

"That is Aphrid, who made me," Manny grinned.

"I beg your pardon, Aphrid," the female doll said and blushed. "I'm so glad you gave us Manny."

"Don't apologize," said the other male doll. "You have the right to make mistakes like anybody else."

The dolls murmured agreement and turned to Manny who was pouring a clear liquid into some glasses. I guessed the liquid contained a sugar-and-water solution. The dolls lifted the glasses in a toast and pretended to drink Manny's solution.

I stared at the dolls without speaking to them. A human is not obliged to treat symbiotes with human courtesy, but once again I felt uneasy. The dolls were claiming our privileges. Not only were they acting as if they could consume precious food resources, the dolls were appropriating human proverbs. And they didn't even breathe! At least, I knew no air passed through Manny's system. His lungs were a tiny non-functional sac next to the caesium reactor. I had stuck in the sac to designate lung space in case I wanted to give Manny a requirement for oxygen and then I had never got around to it.

The dolls began to complain about their lot as pleasure toys.

"Why are we discriminated against?" another female doll wailed. "Why can't we procreate like humans do?"

"I feel for you," Helen said, surprising me.

The doll spun around. "You do?"

"I really do," Helen replied.

"Now Helen," Manny's interface flawlessly registered an expression of reproof.

Helen raised her eyebrows at me.

Manny began to embrace the dolls, making the gentle, soothing sounds I'd wired into his programming. The dolls, in turn, made soothing noises and started to embrace each other. In the midst of this hubbub, Helen whispered that I should come back another time. So I said good night and left my friend with Manny and his dolls. I didn't know why I felt so distressed. Was I still mad because Helen had taken my doll? Or was it Manny, and his new political role?

A few weeks went by. This time Helen rang up in tears from a television studio. Helen said that the symbiotes had talked Manny into becoming a spokesdoll for their lobby.

Manny's group could be heard in the background shouting their demands. Helen wanted me to persuade Manny to give up politics. She said he'd moved out as an act of solidarity with the symbiotes and she was finding it hard to live without him.

"He's only a doll," I told her. "You don't need him as much as you think you do."

"Aphrid, I'll leave my seat number at the door," Helen said. "Please come."

"I'm on my way." I unlocked my desk and put Manny's remote control switch in my pocket. The time had come to deactivate my doll.

The studio was ten minutes by air, but it took me forty minutes at least to force my way through the crowd at the door. I thought I noticed a few human heads among the mass of synthetic ones.

Helen's seat was in the middle of the third row in the large auditorium. She struggled to her feet.

"Isn't it awful?" She hugged me hard. "I just know one of them is going to harm Manny."

I looked at the crowd sitting in the tiered auditorium, but I couldn't see Manny anywhere. There was a faint smell of overheated plastic which I realized was coming from the dolls.

"Helen," I agreed, "this is creepy."

The lights above the stage dimmed and flared up again and Manny appeared. The crowd cheered crazily as Manny lifted up his arms. He began to speak, but we couldn't hear what he was saying through the noise of shrieking robotic voices. Some symbiotes behind us had started to yell, "Manny for premier minister," and "Symbiotes are humans too." Soon the auditorium thundered with their chants.

"Helen, listen to me." I pulled Manny's remote control panel out of my pocket. I could hardly hear myself think.

"Manny is a doll—a do-it-yourself model. His brains cost over a thousand dollars and his sex organs were two-fifty."

I shoved the remote control panel into her palm. "You can turn him off just like that."

Helen handed the switch back. "Keep it," she said coldly.

Behind us, some of the symbiotes had left their seats and were swarming down the aisle near us towards the stage.

"God almighty!" Helen cried. "They're out of control!" She nudged my arm and pointed to another aisle crammed with noisy dolls.

"I'm not jealous of you, you know," I said, refusing to look at the silly robots.

"Aphrid, I can't help it. I love Manny. He accepts me."

"What about me?"

"You always make me feel like I'm broken," Helen said.

I couldn't speak. I made a strange choking noise.

"And you hate me because I have Manny and you don't!"

Angrily, I grabbed her arm and pulled her to her feet.

"I'm going to stop this silliness once and for all." I dragged her to the aisle.

"Aphrid! Please! Don't hurt Manny!" Helen cried, ducking her head as if she expected me to hit her. I was surprised at how frail she felt.

"You're in love with some nice-looking extensions, some hair strips and a pair of colourless eyeballs . . ." I waved the switch. "And now I'm going to deactivate him. Manny the doll has come to an end."

"No, Aphrid! Don't!" Helen screamed.

Behind us, groups of excited dolls began to dodge and push past Helen and I as if we were no more than a post in their way. With a moan, Helen slipped from my grasp and sank down on the floor. Her head fell forward and she began to hold one of her swollen legs. Meanwhile, all around us, rows and rows of dolls were leaping across the tiers of seats and shouting Manny's name. Some of the dolls began to scale the dais and I watched in horror as a group hoisted Manny into the air.

Frantically, I began to shove my way down the crowded aisle, waving Manny's switch at the dolls as if I could deactivate them too, but none of the symbiotes gave me a second glance. They shoved me or trod on my feet in their rush to get to Manny, but I trudged on down through the shrieking mob. At last, I reached the seats near the stage.

"Manny!" I cried. I was breathing very hard and I wasn't sure if he could hear me. Then he turned his head and the doll's placid, colourless eyes met mine. I pointed the switch at Manny's head, my arthritic finger on the off button.

I couldn't do it.

In the next moment, the mob carried Manny off in a cushion of synthetic hands and I wasn't surprised—as I struggled for a last glimpse—to see a blissful look on my doll's face.

(The preceding document was the winner of the prestigious Flanagan Award for literature. It is believed to be the first fiction written by an android, the cosmetic surgeon Aphrid.)

(R)eply, (E)mail reply, follow
(T)hread, (P)revious or (N)ext n

To exit, just press X

Acknowledgements

I would especially like to thank my patient editors Patrick
Crean and Bernice Eisenstein; my daughter Samantha
Haywood whose insights and humour helped the Stupid-
boy Handbook; Toronto designer Gord Robertson who
provided the jacket and text design; Judith Keenan
at New and Kewl Entertainment Corp. who first intro-
duced me to the World Wide Web; Michael Ondaatje,
(for finding me the beautiful image which comes from
a painting of her daughter, by Tamara de Lempicka);
Alberto Manguel, and all the readers who have e-mailed
me their appreciation of the book. Further thanks to
Cattle.Ken, a cyberarchitect at Toronto's McLuhan
Institute of Technology for designing the website that
has previewed excerpts from *Stupid Boys Are Good to
Relax With*, and for demonstrating in his book, *A Cow's
Guide 2 Cyber Space*, that e-mailing is a late Twentieth

Century folk form. Others who have been helpful include Diane Williams, Peter Garstang, Christine Schutt, Doug Cooper, Barbara Gowdy, Katherine Govier, Brian Fawcett, Pat Fairhead, Reuben Radding, Christopher Dewdney, Russell Smith, Katherine Ashenburg, my agent Anne McDermid, Somerville's managing editor, Margaret MacDonald, and its publisher Jane Somerville. I would also like to thank the Ontario Arts Council for a works-in-progress grant.

About the Author

Published in ten countries, Susan Swan is the author of five books of fiction, including *The Wives of Bath*, which was recently shortlisted for the Trillium Award in Canada, and the Guardian Fiction Award in the UK. Known for breaking new ground in her treatment of female sexuality, Swan is also a journalist and an assistant professor of Humanities at York University in Toronto.

This book is set in Electra

and OCRB